What Is Philosophy?

Henry W. Johnstone, Jr.

THE PENNSYLVANIA STATE UNIVERSITY

Sources in Philosophy

A MACMILLAN SERIES

Lewis White Beck, General Editor

THE MACMILLAN COMPANY, NEW YORK

First Printing

Library of Congress catalog card number: 65-11068

THE MACMILLAN COMPANY, NEW YORK

COLLIER-MACMILLAN CANADA, LTD., TORONTO, ONTARIO

Printed in the United States of America

FOR H., A., AND B.

Preface

Answers to the question "What Is Philosophy?" can no doubt be supplied from every period of the history of philosophy. But because the question itself seems to me to be especially urgent in our own time, I have used only contemporary answers as reading selections. In my Introduction I sketch some of the older views of the nature of philosophy, and in my Selected Bibliography at the end of the book I mention some material illustrating these views, as well as some further contemporary items.

For suggestions I am indebted to J. M. Anderson, L. W. Beals, H. A. Finch, E. H. Freund, G. L. Kline, J. C. Morrison, J. A. Mourant, M. Natanson, R. Price, R. M. Rorty, S. H. Rosen, and D. Whittier. The editorial advice and help of both Lewis W. Beck, general editor of this series, and John D. Moore of the Macmillan Company have been of great value to me. I appreciate the secretarial assistance given me by my daughters.

H. W. J., JR.

University Park, Penna.

Contents

Introduction

Let us imagine that a new field of inquiry called Tripology has recently come into existence. A tripologist who wished to introduce his field to college students might compile an anthology entitled *What Is Tripology?* In this book we would expect to find an introductory section in which a standard definition of Tripology is presented, perhaps one taken from the writings of an eminent tripologist. In fact, several such definitions might be quoted. In any event, the introductory section would be followed by readings illustrating the various branches of Tripology, its various techniques, and its various applications to other sciences and to everyday life. These readings would constitute the main substance of the book. No responsible tripologist wishing to acquaint others with his field would omit them and compile an anthology consisting wholly of definitions of Tripology. He would regard a collection of definitions as neither necessary nor sufficient for his purpose. The definitions are unnecessary because any intelligent reader could learn what Tripology is about by skipping immediately to the main part of the book. And they are certainly by no means sufficient: a person who had merely read several definitions of Tripology would still be far from understanding how tripological results are obtained. In other words, the initial definition of Tripology is really a kind of luxury. Textbooks, to be sure, have always opened with definitions, but perhaps this is largely a formality.

While no one would attempt to introduce Tripology by offering only a collection of definitions of the field, there are strong reasons for introducing philosophy in just this way. Unlike the intelligent reader who has skipped the definitions of Tripology, a reader confronted with a group of philosophical writings might not be able to see in what way they were all contributions to a single field even though he understood the writings in themselves well enough. In order to know what to look for in the writings, he would need a definition. Thus one difference between philosophy and Tripology is that a definition of philosophy can be much more illuminating than one of Tripology. But there is another difference as well. While tripologists may clash over definitions of Tripology, their disagreements are not likely to be as radical as those that philosophers have over the definition of philosophy. Suppose a reputable tripologist named Jones has offered a definition of his field. His colleagues may object that his definition is too broad, that it includes inquiries that properly belong to a neighboring field. Or they may judge it to be too narrow. But they are extremely unlikely to say: "Jones has completely the wrong idea of the nature of Tripology. What he calls Tripology is just not Tripology at all. He doesn't grasp the true purposes of Tripology. He has no notion of what its proper method is. In fact, Jones's view of the nature of Tripology is altogether dangerous. It could lead to the collapse of public morals and the subversion of responsible government—it may even be a threat to the future of civilization." If his colleagues said things like that about him, Jones would not be a reputable tripologist. But reputable philosophers could reasonably say exactly such things about each other. Each of two equally competent philosophers may accuse the other of altogether missing the point of philosophy, of not knowing how to philosophize properly, and of propagating dangerous nonsense. Even when there are no explicit confrontations of this sort, it is obvious from the radically different ways in which philosophers have defined their field what the accusations would be.

It follows that if a group of examples of philosophy were preceded by no more than a single definition of philosophy, even the reader who found this definition illuminating might be properly suspicious of it. He might wonder what radically different definitions were being withheld from him. As soon as he begins to entertain such suspicions, he will see that *examples* of philosophy constitute a much less satisfactory introduction to the field than *definitions* of philosophy. This is why it is reasonable to compile an anthology entitled *What Is Philosophy?* composed entirely of answers to this question.

Radical disagreements over the definition of philosophy might be taken as clear evidence of the irrationality of both the philosophers and their field. Reasonable investigators in the same field, it might be argued, ought to be able to agree about what it is they are investigating and how to investigate it. What this objection overlooks, however, is the difference between the situation in which the definition of a field is a necessity and that in which it is a luxury. We need not define Tripology because the examples themselves show clearly enough what the tripologist is concerned with and how he goes about his inquiries. Thus it is not quite accurate to say that there is general agreement on the definition of Tripology: There is neither agreement nor disagreement, but rather a casual and relaxed attitude toward the whole question of definition; it is regarded as largely an academic question. Yet the question might arise in a more urgent form. Recent advances in a number of studies have raised questions regarding the definitions of these fields. Thus "What is physics (as distinct from chemistry)?" "What is history (a social science or one of the humanities)?" and "What is psychiatry (in relation to psychology)?" are legitimate requests for definitions of various disciplines. Concerning the definitions supplied in response to these requests, two points should be noted. In the first place, the question "What is physics?" is not a question within physics, the question "What is history?" is not a historical question, and the question "What is psychiatry?" is not a question to which psychiatry itself can provide the answer. All are, in fact, *philosophical* questions. In the second place, there has been no general agreement on the answers to these questions. The dispute as to whether history is a social science or one of the humanities rages in academic assemblies to this day. These two points are in fact closely related. Philosophical positions, including philosophical definitions of fields, are always controversial. This is true even of the attempt to define philosophy itself. For this attempt too is philosophical. Although the questions "What is Tripology?" and "What is physics?" do not belong to these fields themselves, the question "What is philosophy?" is itself a philosophical question. This is why we should expect any answer to it to be controversial.

I

The origin of the word *philosopher* is instructive. When the Greek thinker Pythagoras (572–497 B.C.) was asked whether he regarded himself as a wise man, he modestly replied that he was not wise, but merely a lover of wisdom; and the Greek for *lover of wisdom* is *philosophos,* whence our word *philosopher.* The suggestion is that philosophy is nothing but the pursuit of wisdom, and thus if we had the wisdom itself there would be no need to maintain the pursuit. What wisdom itself might be Pythagoras did not tell us, but we can imagine it as a kind of absolute knowledge, completely beyond disagreement and doubt. Plato (428–348 B.C.) used the figure of the Divided Line to symbolize this distinction between absolute knowledge and beliefs that are doubtful and subject to disagreement. He placed the kind of knowledge the philosopher seeks at the top of his figure and mathematics just below it. In these two types of knowledge man has access to the world of reality. Below them, and separated from them as appearance is separated from reality, Plato placed all beliefs affected by doubt and disagreement. Hence any disagreement would be a sure sign that the parties to it had not achieved wisdom. In other passages Plato was careful to point out that philosophical disagreement plays an indispensable role in our pursuit of wisdom; without *dialectic*, or philosophical discussion in which our disagreements are progressively resolved, we can never hope to attain wisdom at all. But it is clear that philosophical discussion is not itself wisdom; it is only a means of attaining it and would be superfluous if it were ever completely attained.

Aristotle (384–322 B.C.) regarded the wisdom sought in philosophy as properly belonging to God, but occasionally available to men. Aristotle's scale of the degrees of cognition, unlike Plato's Divided Line, does not suggest that wisdom is altogether different in kind from what humans ordinarily claim to know. It is just the most general, the most precise, and the most difficult kind of knowledge. Yet Aristotle seems to agree with Plato that philosophy is no more than the way to achieve wisdom. Plato and Aristotle both expressed the relation between man's original innocence and the wisdom he may be led to seek by saying that philosophy begins in "wonder." If so, it ends in the extinction of wonder.

In the Middle Ages philosophy was considered the handmaiden of theology. It was a means of ascertaining the truths about God that are accessible to unaided human reason. Since it was supposed that not all theological truths *are* accessible to human reason, but that some of them can be learned only through revelation, philosophy had a humbler role for medieval thinkers than it had had for the Greeks. Not only was it merely a means to knowledge, but it was a means to merely a part of knowledge--to the part that could be acquired through reason.

René Descartes (1596–1650) is regarded as the founder of modern philosophy. He felt that philosophy in his own day had fallen to a disgraceful state:

> Of Philosophy I will say nothing, except that when I saw that it had been cultivated for many ages by the most distinguished men, and that yet there is not a single matter within its sphere which is not still in dispute, and nothing, therefore, which is above doubt, I did not presume to anticipate that my success would be greater in it than that of others.[1]

In his *Discourse on Method* he proposed a remedy in the form of rules for conducting an investigation. Three of these rules are:

> . . . never to accept anything for true which I did not clearly know to be such . . . ;
>
> . . . to divide each of the difficulties under examination into as many parts as possible, and as might be necessary for its adequate solution;
>
> . . . to conduct my thoughts in such order that, by commencing with objects the simplest and easiest to know, I might ascend . . . as it were, step by step, to the knowledge of the more complex.[2]

It is clear from these rules that Descartes' model for any investigation, including a philosophical one, was a mathematical model. The use of a mathematical model for philosophical inquiry becomes explicit in the writings of Spinoza (1632–1677), whose philosophical system took the form of a set of theorems supposedly deduced from some fundamental axioms, postulates, and definitions. Spinoza also suggested in some of his writings that what he regarded as the goal of philosophy was similar to the Greek conception of wisdom. In any event, Descartes and Spinoza were both explicitly thinking of philosophy as a mathematical or supermathematical device for achieving absolutely certain results.

In the Preface to his *Critique of Pure Reason* Immanuel Kant (1724–1804) complained, in much the same vein as Descartes, about the lack of progress in traditional philosophy. But instead of proceeding by attempting to reduce philosophy to a supermathematics,

[1] John Veitch (trans.), *The Method, Meditations, and Philosophy of Descartes* (New York: Tudor Publishing Co., n.d.), pp. 153–154.

[2] *Ibid.*, p. 161.

Kant's approach was to examine the conditions under which knowledge is possible. Primary among these, he asserted, was the condition that the objects of knowledge must fall within the bounds of the objects of possible experience. He found that while science and mathematics meet this condition, traditional philosophy does not, and this is why it must remain controversial. Problems about God, human freedom, the immortality of the soul, the beginning of the world, the infinity of space, and so on, cannot be solved, Kant declared, in terms of any possible experience. Yet by his very nature man must be concerned with these problems.

We may summarize the views surveyed so far by saying that until the time of Kant philosophy had been regarded as a way of getting knowledge or wisdom, and hence as something that we could do without if its goal were known to be unattainable, or if there were an easier way of attaining the wisdom that is its goal. Kant denied that philosophy is a way of getting knowledge at all. Of course, this suspicion had been entertained many times before; the pretensions of philosophers have been ridiculed ever since Aristophanes satirized Socrates in *The Clouds*. But Kant was the first to see the frustrated yearning for philosophical truth as a central fact about human nature rather than as the foible of a few maladjusted people.

G. W. F. Hegel (1770–1831) agreed with Kant that the urge to philosophize is basic to human nature, but argued that this urge is in no way a defect even though its results are inherently controversial. For Hegel rejected Kant's view that philosophy has never made any progress. Even though no philosophical view has ever won final acceptance, and even if none ever will, there is progress from any view to its successor. In the act of criticizing old philosophies, new philosophies arise that are more subtle, more sophisticated, and more articulate than their predecessors. Furthermore, Hegel saw philosophy as both the foundation and the reflection of civilization. The history of philosophy is an expression of the history of civilization, and vice versa. Philosophy, then, is an autonomous force, unfolding itself through history as the direct result of the controversial quality of each of its own formulations; and this is the driving force of Hegel's world.

II

There is no general agreement among contemporary thinkers as to the role of philosophy. Some regard philosophy as the pursuit of knowledge of one sort or another and would argue that if the fruits of this pursuit are genuinely controversial, then the pursuit has to that extent failed. Others, including the logical positivists and many of the linguistic analysts, hold that what the traditional philosopher pursues is not knowledge but pseudoknowledge: since the problems he is trying to solve are not real problems, the attempt to solve them is just a mistake. This attitude toward philosophy is somewhat like Kant's except that the positivists and linguistic analysts have not regarded the urge to philosophize as a built-in feature of human nature. They have thought instead that man might be purified or cured of this urge. Other philosophers insist that philosophy is a legitimate enterprise even if its results must always be controversial. We will meet all these positions, and others, in the readings that follow.

The selection from Jacques Maritain, a piece of contemporary writing, actually illustrates the medieval view of the nature of philosophy. Maritain unequivocally declares that philosophy consists in knowing. He thinks of it as a science—not one that absorbs or competes with the other sciences, but a *universal* science, concerned with the most fundamental causes of phenomena.[3] The other sciences study causes of a less remote and more immediately effective nature. For example, while the biologist tries to explain how animals move, and the physicist is interested in the question of how molecules, atoms, and subatomic particles move, the philosopher asks why there should be motion at all. The existence of motion is one of the unexamined presuppositions on which some of the sciences rest. Other such presuppositions are the existence of space, time, matter, life, and mind. Each of the special sciences has some presuppositions that it does not itself examine. It is the business of philosophy to carry out this examination.

[3] In the terminology of the philosopher, a *phenomenon* (pl. *phenomena*) is anything that appears to exist or any event that has seemed to occur, regardless of whether it really does exist or really has occurred.

Although his language may strike some ears as strange, adapted as it is from that of the medieval philosopher St. Thomas Aquinas (1225–1274), Maritain is actually expressing a view that has wide currency nowadays. Philosophers of many different persuasions agree that philosophy is concerned with the presuppositions of science as well as with whatever is presupposed in activities of other kinds: morals, politics, art, and so on. For example, morals presupposes the concepts of right and wrong, politics the concept of civil obedience, and art the concept of aesthetic unity, and philosophy examines all such concepts. Presuppositions may take the form not only of concepts but also of fundamental beliefs: every event has a cause, it is never right to lie, civil disobedience is sometimes right. The task of the philosopher, in this view, is to express presupposed concepts and beliefs accurately and clearly, to ascertain which of the beliefs are true and which false, and if possible to define some of the concepts in terms of others of them and to derive the true beliefs from more fundamental ones.

If such is the goal of philosophy, then the philosopher will not want to restrict himself to any one method. He expects to be judged not by the way in which he has performed his task, but by his success or failure in performing it—by whether he has succeeded in clarifying the concepts and establishing the truth or falsity of the beliefs with which he was concerned. To ask him to perform this difficult and abstruse task by some one method or some restricted set of methods is like asking a surgeon to perform a delicate operation with only a single surgical instrument. To be sure, Maritain asserts that the philosopher must use *reason*. But reason in itself is scarcely a method: it is, rather, a name for a large variety of methods. The axiomatic method of Descartes and the dialectical method of Plato both involve the use of reason, and so do many other methods as well.

Not all philosophers, however, agree with Maritain that there is a science [4] to which philosophy is subservient. For Maritain this higher science is theology. Philosophy is merely the highest *human* science; and above it is a science that could be perfectly practiced only by God. To the extent that theology extends beyond the region

[4] By "science" Maritain means any systematic body of knowledge. This is a common usage among philosophers of a number of different schools of thought.

of philosophical truths, its truths are available to humans only in the form of revelation. Notice, however, that Maritain does not maintain that all uses of philosophy are subservient to theology. When philosophy is not concerned with theological questions, it can freely pursue its own goals.

Although Bertrand Russell's philosophical position differs from Maritain's in nearly every detail, Russell still shares with Maritain an underlying attitude regarding the relation between philosophy and method. In spite of the title of his essay "Scientific Method in Philosophy," Russell is not proposing that the philosopher commit himself to any one method. Russell is using the phrase "scientific method" in much the same way as Maritain uses "reason"; viz., to refer to a large number of methods any one of which is proper insofar as it produces results of the relevant kind. What Russell says in specifying this kind of results also reminds one of Maritain. Philosophical results, as opposed to scientific ones must be *general.* (Maritain uses the term "universal.") They must also be a priori; that is, concerned with what could possibly exist and with what must necessarily exist rather than with what actually does exist. Philosophy is the science of the possible. In this role, says Russell, it is indistinguishable from logic. In saying this Russell is still not recommending the exclusive use of any one method in philosophy. "Logic" does not mean, for example, axiomatic method. It means instead a broad concern for the forms of statements and for statements that are true by virtue of their forms alone—"general statements," as Russell calls them here. He gives examples of these objects of the logician's concern.

Russell himself would be the first to insist that logic is not a skeleton key that fits all philosophical problems. Various philosophical problems can be solved by means of logic, but in each case the logical key must be constructed to fit the lock. This piecemeal approach to philosophical problems is characteristic of what Russell means by "analysis." Philosophical analysis runs counter to the traditional notion that a philosophy should be constructed all in one block, and that if not wholly correct it is wholly incorrect. Like the sciences, philosophical analysis can be tentative and can solve part of a problem at a time. Russell illustrates this approach in terms of "the" problem of space. His first step is to show that three problems are involved instead of just one. He goes about solving each problem in its own terms, rather than attempting to apply any general method to all three.

When we reach the Rudolf Carnap selection we are confronted with an attitude toward philosophical problems radically different from that of Maritain or Russell. Carnap's position is known as logical positivism. While Russell has doubts about the solvability of some traditional philosophical problems, Carnap is generally suspicious about the possibility of solving any of them. He dismisses them wholesale rather than attempting to solve them in a piecemeal way. He justifies this wholesale dismissal by defining philosophy in a strictly limited way. The only legitimate task of philosophy, according to Carnap, is to formulate the logical syntax of the sciences.

We can best explain the phrase "logical syntax" by outlining the considerations that lead Carnap to use it. Carnap asserts that questions of only two types arise in any theoretical field. *Object questions* are concerned with the objects dealt with in the field, for example, animals, plants, stars, or atoms, depending on the science we are considering. "Do all whales suckle their young?" would be an object question in zoology. *Logical questions* have to do with the forms (in Russell's sense) of the statements within a given science and with the logical relations among such statements. Thus "All whales suckle their young" is a statement having a certain recognizable logical form and is related in a definite logical way to the two statements "All mammals suckle their young" and "All whales are mammals." Now consider the question "Are whales fish?" This might be taken as an object-question: perhaps in order to answer it we ought to examine whales and see if they have the characteristics of fish. But this is not the only way the question can be taken. Suppose we know clearly what is meant by "whale" and what is meant by "fish." Then the question we have to answer is only: How are "whale" and "fish" logically related? This logical question falls within what Carnap calls "logical syntax." Logical syntax is always relative to a particular scientific language that includes certain terms and excludes others, and for which there are precise rules telling us what combinations of words make sense and what combinations do not.

Now why does Carnap identify the proper business of philosophy as logical syntax? He complains that in the past what has been called philosophy has in fact consisted of a mixture of object-questions and logical questions. The object-questions that have exercised philosophers either concern so-called objects that are not in fact locatable as objects dealt with in any of the sciences, or else they are inquiries about objects found in the sciences. In the latter case, of course, the inquiry itself should be conducted within the relevant science rather than in philosophy. Hence when Descartes used philosophical arguments in the effort to determine whether a vacuum is possible, he was misconceiving the nature of the question, which is actually an object-question of physics. Now consider philosophical object-questions that are not scientific object-questions: "Does God exist?" "Is the world nothing more than my idea?" and "Are there such things as Intelligence, Citizenship, and the Number 4 as well as ordinary things?" Some of these Carnap refuses to regard as real questions at all. They are just pseudoquestions, springing from the mistaken belief that there are objects inaccessible to science—objects like "God," "the world," and so on. But other questions that at least seem to be philosophical object-questions come off better in his treatment. These are the logical questions in disguise; that is, the ones that can be translated into questions about logical syntax and then answered in a definite way. Thus the question about Intelligence, Citizenship, and the Number 4 can be interpreted as an inquiry not about things at all but about the kinds of words allowable in a particular scientific language—perhaps that of a formulation of political science. In the Carnap selection a number of such translations will be found. They all illustrate his contention that since philosophy has no legitimate concern with scientific object-questions, and since nonscientific ones are really only pseudoquestions, all that philosophy can properly occupy itself with is logical syntax. It goes without saying that the role Carnap envisages for philosophy is a humble one. There is, he asserts, no such thing as a peculiarly philosophical standpoint from which to view the sciences. And no correct philosophical utterance can be absolute; it can be no more than relative to a particular scientific language.

Thus the task Carnap proposes for philosophy is strictly limited.

Such a limited task naturally invites the use of a restricted method; for if we proceed unmethodically, we will achieve our restricted goals only by chance if at all. Carnap's method should now be clear. He translates philosophical problems either into object-questions of science, which he hands over to the scientist to answer, or into questions about logical syntax. When neither kind of translation is possible (as Carnap and other logical positivists believe is often the case in metaphysics and ethics), he rejects them as pseudoproblems and regards the answers to them as no more than the disguised expressions of emotions. In its reliance on such a method, Carnap's approach is profoundly different from the essentially unmethodical approach of Russell.

The selection from Max Black's *Language and Philosophy* is a lucid example of the method of linguistic analysis. The main difference between this position and Carnap's logical positivism is that the linguistic emphasis is upon ordinary language, not upon the language of science. Black feels that many philosophical problems —perhaps all—arise from a misunderstanding of the ways in which ordinary words are used and of the relationships among such words. He illustrates this thesis by analyzing the suggestion, often made by philosophers, that what is in a person's mind may be literally incommunicable. Perhaps my experience of colors is radically different from that of other people, so that what I experience when I look at a green object is what others experience when looking at a red object. Or maybe some other individual is color-blind in a way that neither he nor I can detect, because we both respond behaviorally in exactly the same way to different colors. Black explores this suggestion. Color-blindness, he points out, is defined by behavioral tests. It consists in a difference between the color response of the color-blind person and that of normal people. In practice the tests may be crude and unformulated. But the meaning of the term "color-blind" does not presuppose that any sharp and clearly defined test exists. It only presupposes that the test could be specified if necessary. Hence the sceptic who claims that the color-blind person and the normal person *might* respond in exactly the same way to the same colors has contradicted himself, and it is impossible to know what he means. He is using the term "color-blind" in what Black calls a "limiting sense." While we can set up tests for increasingly subtle cases of color-blindness, we cannot set up a test for an *infinitely* subtle case of it.

When Black suggests that philosophers often distort the meanings of terms by using them in a limiting sense, he is perfectly right. Many philosophers have typically used terms in such a way that there can be no test to determine the correctness or incorrectness of their application. Thus when Leibniz (1646–1716) said "All is for the best in this best of possible worlds," he was presumably using the adjective "best" in a limiting sense. Black himself provides other examples: knowledge of the future, conceived as such perfect knowledge that it would never need to be revised; and the human soul, conceived as wholly distinct from the bodily or mental properties of the person. But it can be argued that philosophy can make legitimate use of the limiting sense of words, and that in attempting to eliminate this sense, Black is actually threatening to do away with philosophy altogether. Alfred North Whitehead (1861–1947) once wrote that philosophy deals with concepts that "cannot fail of exemplification"; and we may remind ourselves that in saying that philosophy is "a priori," Russell had much the same thing in mind. Indeed Black himself seems to be saying that most of what has gone under the name of philosophy, if not all of it, involves the limiting sense of concepts. Certainly all the problems he considers at the outset—problems about free will, the reality of time, the existence of other minds and the external world, the possibility of knowledge about the future or about matters of fact—can be regarded as arising from this source. But if such problems had never come into existence, one wonders whether the method of linguistic analysis recommended by Black could have come into existence either. Is Black fundamentally interested in philosophizing, or in doing away with philosophy? Ludwig Wittgenstein (1889–1951), one of the founders of the linguistic method, whose influence on Black is obvious, said quite explicitly that the purpose of his reflections was to enable him to give up philosophizing.

While Black is in effect proposing to revise Carnap's position, by shifting the basis of analysis from scientific to ordinary language, Maurice Cornforth introduces his account of the nature of philosophy with a vigorous attack on everything Carnap has stood for. He accuses the logical positivists of subverting philosophy by rejecting its classical aim to give an account of the world and of man. In relegating object-questions to particular sciences, and in thus reducing philosophy to an analysis of language, the positivists have cut philosophy off from science as well as from life. But "what is required of philosophy is rather that it should draw its principles and conclusions from the sciences themselves."

Cornforth is expressing a common enough complaint about logical positivism, and if we were to assess his position solely on the basis of his attack on Carnap, we would find it difficult to distinguish it from many other philosophical positions current today. As we read further in the Cornforth selection, however, we become aware that his position has a quite distinctive structure; namely, that of contemporary Marxism. Although Cornforth is an Englishman, the point of view he expresses is in all essential respects identical with the current Soviet doctrine regarding the nature of philosophy. Marxism, of course, whether English or Soviet, derives from the philosophy of the German thinker Karl Marx (1818–1883).

Marxism is an example of a more general philosophical point of view known as naturalism.[5] According to naturalism, all human values and achievements can be sufficiently explained in terms of nature. Human history is a natural process; it is merely an extension of the natural process of organic evolution. It is because he thinks of science as precisely the knowledge of nature that the Marxist insists that philosophy must draw its principles and conclusions from science. Among the scientific data he regards as most important to the philosopher are those concerning the rise and fall of social classes in the process of human history. According to Marxism, the first distinctive social class to emerge in historical times was the feudal aristocracy. But that class carried within it "the seeds of its own destruction"; it eventually gave rise to the mercantile class, or bourgeoisie. This class, in turn, has produced the proletariat, that is, the workers who will one day inherit the world.

Philosophers, according to Cornforth, are products of their times. One result of the bourgeois revolt against feudalism, for example, was to replace a comfortable philosophy, according to which everything in the universe had its proper place and every event served

[5] Actually, Marxism identifies itself as "dialectical materialism." Materialism, the belief that matter alone is ultimately real, is, of course, a type of naturalism.

a purpose, with the harsher view that in an infinite universe it makes no sense to speak of the "proper place" of anything, and that every event can be explained in purely mechanical terms, without regard to purpose. Of course it was this bourgeois view that made modern science possible. But the bourgeoisie did not reach this view through free inquiry; its outlook "was itself determined, formed, and bounded by the new social relations within which the philosophers were confined." The question whether the pronouncements of the Marxist philosopher are not themselves, by his own principles, determined by their social milieu seems irresistible. But the Marxist has a ready answer: In his feudal and bourgeois existence, man is estranged from his own true nature; he is not free because he has become a victim of systematic delusions. But as a proletarian, man returns to himself, and having recovered his full humanity, he is free.

The selection from John Dewey is concerned with many issues that have already been touched on. Dewey, like Black, believes that philosophy traditionally has used concepts in such a way as to render intelligent discussion impossible. In attempting to present the truth in the form of a complete logical system, it has ignored ordinary experience and everyday facts. But unlike Black, Dewey gives a sociological account of these hyperlogical pretensions. He says that they stem from a legitimate need to reconcile social institutions and beliefs with facts and with change. Thus Plato's philosophy sprang from the attempt to maintain what is best in a traditionally accepted aristocracy in the face of the great social unrest of his own time. The result, among other things, was a belief in timeless essences which are wholly distinct from the facts of ordinary life. In this selection and elsewhere Dewey gives similar explanations of most of the great philosophical systems and movements. Notice that unlike the Marxists, Dewey does not suppose that philosophy is determined by class structure. It is always a free product of creativity. But in each case it is an attempt to conserve social values.

If we were to substitute "vested interests" for "social values" in the last sentence, we would have the expression of a plausible cynicism regarding the function of philosophy. But Dewey does not share this cynicism. For he believes that philosophy can be the conservator of what is genuinely valuable in social traditions. Progress from primitive to modern culture has depended on two conditions: clashes of social ends and the philosophical clarification that has overcome such clashes, retaining what is best in each of the conflicting institutions. "The task of future philosophy," says Dewey, "is to clarify men's ideas as to the social and moral strife of their own day."

Dewey not only offers an alternative to cynicism regarding the function of philosophy, but also avoids the scepticism [6] that seems inherent in the linguistic method recommended by Black. To the extent that philosophy aims at expounding a hyperlogical truth, transcending the facts of ordinary experience, it can perhaps justly be accused of dealing in the limiting senses of concepts, and hence in self-contradictory notions. But Dewey is suggesting that such intellectualistic concerns are not the true *raison d'être* of philosophy. Philosophy is essentially a social transaction, the success or failure of which does not depend upon the intellectual coinage in terms of which it is effected. Thus Dewey sidesteps scepticism by changing the venue of the problem from the intellectual to the social.

It is obvious that in the very act of defining philosophy Dewey is in effect proposing a method for it. Philosophical problems, he is saying, ought to be solved in social terms. If a problem reflects a social conflict, then its solution must be such as to reduce or eliminate the conflict. Dewey, then, like Carnap and Black, is one of the philosophers who envisage the goals of philosophy in a sufficiently restricted way to make the use of a method fruitful. Another such philosopher is Edmund Husserl. Like Dewey, too, Husserl wishes to avoid scepticism with regard to the possibility of achieving success in philosophy. But in other respects Husserl's view is altogether unlike Dewey's.

With Husserl we come once more to a view that philosophical problems are purely intellectual. Husserl's goal, in fact, is to make

[6] Scepticism is primarily the view that there are questions human beings cannot answer, because the answers lie beyond the scope of man's limited powers. In a derivative sense the view that the questions themselves are meaningless—a view taken by Carnap as well as by Black with respect to some of the important questions dealt with in traditional philosophy—may be regarded as scepticism.

philosophy into a "strict science." Alleged solutions to philosophical problems are to be judged not by their social consequences, or by consequences of any other kind. They are to be judged simply in terms of their conformity to the standards of a strict science. In other words, they must constitute genuine items of knowledge of an unquestionable kind. We are reminded here of the way in which Descartes visualized the task of the philosopher. In fact, Husserl thoroughly approves of the spirit of Descartes's approach.

An example of a "strict science" in Husserl's sense is classical mechanics as founded by Galileo and completed by Newton. Husserl points out that in comparison with such a science, philosophy not only never has been a strict science—it has not been a science at all. There are basic scientific truths, which no one disputes. But there are no philosophical statements that are not subject to dispute. One very important reason, according to Husserl, why philosophy has lacked the foundations expected in a science is that it has attempted to build on foundations borrowed from other sciences—in particular, from the natural sciences. The natural sciences are defined by a fundamental concern with nature. But when philosophers assume that they too are fundamentally concerned with nature, their conclusions are paradoxical and controversial. Among the results of such improper philosophizing are what Husserl calls "the naturalizing of consciousness" and "the naturalizing of ideas." Both of these errors are exemplified by Marxism, although to be sure that was not Husserl's main target. To naturalize consciousness is to assume that consciousness is part of nature. Those who maintain that consciousness is nothing but physiological activity of a certain sort—that "the brain secretes thought as the liver secretes bile," to quote the zoologist Carl Vogt (1817–1895)—make this assumption in a fairly obvious way. A more subtle form of the assumption is "psychophysical dualism," the doctrine that even though thought and other forms of mental life—emotions, sensations, feelings, and so on—are unique in quality and cannot be reduced to physiological activities, they are nonetheless correlated with such activities in the sense that there is a strict correspondence between stimulus and response. In this form the assumption dominates experimental psychology. Consciousness continues to be naturalized, for mental phenomena are treated as existing in only a secondary way. They continue to be studied from a point of view in which it is never forgotten that they are responses to stimuli that fall within nature.

A most important example of "the naturalizing of ideas" is found in "psychologism," the tendency to regard purposeful and self-controlled thinking as merely a natural phenomenon. Thus the principles of logic are sometimes regarded as psychological laws according to which conclusions of certain forms are naturally associated with premises of certain forms. But this account completely overlooks the fact that logic is concerned not with *natural* thought processes but with *correct* thinking. And if purpose is merely a natural phenomenon, then the philosopher dominated by the purpose of naturalizing consciousness is a paradoxical figure, if not a comic one. His very vigor in advocating his doctrine presupposes that the doctrine has a meaning of which it can itself give no account.

Philosophy can hope to become a strict science only if its foundations are its own and not borrowed from any natural science, including psychology. The nature of these foundations has already been suggested. If philosophical failure results from dealing with mental phenomena as if they existed in a secondary way, success presupposes that they must be thought of as existing in a primary way. The strict philosophical science that is to deal with mental phenomena in this primary way, considering thoughts, emotions, sensations, and feelings each to exist in its own right, is a science Husserl calls *phenomenology*. The root method of phenomenology is *suspension of the natural attitude;* that is, of the attitude we are taking when our judgments presuppose the existence of nature. We take this attitude, for example, when we think of a feeling or a sensation as a *response*. We suspend it when we come to investigate the feeling or sensation in itself, without regard to its being a natural product of any natural stimulus from an existing object. Consider, for example, the mental phenomenon we call "perceiving a material object." In the natural attitude we will obviously interpret such a phenomenon as a sign that we are in the presence of a material object. But if we are to engage in phenomenology we must utterly disregard the question of whether there is in fact a material object present to cause us to perceive; this question, in any particular case, belongs perhaps to psychology, but not to phenomenology. We must concentrate on the perception itself. What is the perception like, and what other types of perception is it related to? What is the sensory content of the perception, and what expectations of further sensory content does it contain? (When I perceive a table, I do not merely see the side of it nearest me, but I also expect that under certain conditions I could see parts of it which I do not now see—and this expectation is part of what it means to perceive the table.) In other words, what is it to perceive a material object? This is a question not about an actual material object, but about any possible perception of one. Husserl would not disagree with Russell's statement that philosophy is the science of the possible, and, like Russell, he refers to it as an a priori discipline. Husserl might well have complained, however, that Russell never in fact clearly departed from the natural standpoint, so that his philosophy is a hodgepodge of elements that are a priori and ones that are not. Husserl for his part was altogether intent on suspending the natural attitude, and the investigations this suspension made possible are the main source of the phenomenological movement which has been of such great importance to contemporary European philosophy.

The authors discussed so far have all either defined philosophy outright (for example, Maritain) or else have said what they take the goal of philosophy to be and what they regard as the best method of achieving this goal. Actually, the second approach results in fully as unambiguous a definition of philosophy as the first. For the endorsement of a method amounts to the same thing as the acceptance of a view of the nature of philosophy. This is clearly the case, for example, with Husserl. It is difficult to imagine applying the phenomenological method he recommends in the service of anything but philosophy as he conceives it—the science of the possible. Similarly Carnap, Black, and Dewey in proposing methods for philosophy are in effect defining philosophy itself. Here is an important difference between philosophy and science. Tripology, our imaginary science that can be taken as any science whatever, has as its goal the investigation of objects of a certain kind. This goal, however, does not prescribe any particular method, except within very broad limits. The methods of astronomy would be inappropriate to the goals of microbiology, but no detailed methods can be deduced from these goals. The goals might be accomplished by a number of different methods, and they can remain fixed while the methods are improved. Nor can the goals of a science be inferred from its methods. In science there is thus a considerable degree of independence between purpose and method. But in philosophy the independence tends to vanish, so that if we know the goal of a philosophy, we are likely to have a fairly good idea what its method must be (or, in the case of thinkers who regard philosophy as simply wisdom or knowledge, we can foretell that there will be a methodical rejection of any restricted and restrictive method), and it would be difficult to be skillful in applying the method of a philosophy without being aware of its goal.

But if a philosopher's view of the goals of philosophy is really as dependent on his view of philosophical method as we have said it is, we seem to be led to a new sceptical impasse. In Tripology, where, presumably, different investigators can use different methods to pursue the same goal, each investigator can criticize the methods of his colleagues as relatively successful or unsuccessful in attaining the common goal. But in philosophy, this kind of criticism is usually not possible, because different investigators are using different methods to pursue *different* goals. Furthermore, the method of each investigator will commit him to denying the legitimacy of the goals of his colleagues. Each will say, in effect, that he alone is philosophizing. An illustration of this total failure to communicate can be obtained by considering what Dewey would say about Husserl's goals and what Husserl would say about Dewey's. What each takes to be the final goals of philosophy will make it possible for him to display the goals of the other as falling short of these final goals.

The predicaments philosophers with different outlooks and methods find themselves in vis-à-vis one another are considered by Richard McKeon in his article "Philosophy and Method." McKeon classifies the myriad of possible philosophical methods under three main headings: dialectic, logistic, and inquiry. Dialectical methods are exemplified by Plato, whose dialectic we have already had occasion to mention, and by the dialectical materialism advocated by the Marxists. The essence of dialectic is its aim to overcome any apparent contradiction by finding a larger whole of which the seemingly contradictory assertions can simultaneously be true. Thus, to take a simple example, roundness is inconsistent with squareness, but a cylinder can be round from one perspective and square from another. Similarly, the issue between two seemingly inconsistent philosophical claims might be resolved by finding a larger whole of which each of the claims is in reality only a view from a certain perspective. Thus a dialectical philosopher would try to reconcile the conflicting assertions of optimism and pessimism, of materialism and idealism, of liberalism and conservatism. When dialectic is the method of a philosophy, its purpose is to unify experience—to find some whole of which all of our experiences merely reveal aspects.

Plato, Hegel, and Marx are perhaps the chief historical exponents of dialectical views, but such views are not very common in contemporary philosophy. The only selection in this book that could be said to represent a recommendation of dialectical method (apart from the Cornforth piece, which does not, however, explicitly deal with the dialectical aspects of Marxism) is the one from Collingwood on which we have not yet commented. Other recent dialectical philosophers have been the American thinker Brand Blanshard (1892–), the Spaniard José Ortega y Gasset (1883–1955), and the Italians Benedetto Croce (1866–1952) and Giovanni Gentile (1875–1944).

Logistic philosophies, falling under McKeon's second main heading, are easier to exemplify in terms already familiar to the reader. Russell and Carnap are both logistic philosophers, and so, in a somewhat different way, is Husserl. Logistic method does not attempt to reconcile disputed propositions; it concerns itself precisely with propositions that are not disputed—the ones that by common consent are regarded as having the status of knowledge. It attempts to trace knowledge back to its simple elements. The mathematical approach of Descartes and Spinoza is an example of logistic method, because the axioms and postulates from which a field of mathematics is derived can be regarded as the simple elements of that field, and Descartes and Spinoza tried to find philosophical axioms and postulates that would correspond with mathematical ones. But a philosopher who espouses the logistic method does not necessarily commit himself to presenting his views in the form of an explicit deductive system. It is sufficient that he should be interested in formulating the elements of knowledge as strict science. Russell is clearly attempting to reduce our knowledge of space to its elements, and the rules of logical syntax are for Carnap among the elements of a scientific language. For Husserl the building blocks of philosophy are the phenomena of consciousness considered in their own right rather than merely as the mental correlates of physical stimuli. Among the elements that other philosophers have sometimes assumed are atoms, "clear and distinct ideas," and immediate sense-experience.

Finally, there are methods of inquiry. These are aimed at solving particular problems one at a time and without reference to an all-inclusive whole or to simplest parts. A solution is regarded as acceptable just so long as it "works." There are various ways of deciding whether the solution to a problem "works," but the reference is usually to action rather than theory. If a problem arises when action of some sort is blocked, the most acceptable solution will be the one that restores action where it is blocked and disturbs it as little as possible elsewhere. William James (1842–1910) and Dewey typify methods of inquiry. To the extent that Dewey recommends the piecemeal solution of problems, so does Black; but of course Black is not much concerned with action.

Philosophies associated with methods of inquiry are likely not only to neglect theory but also to distrust it. They are often anti-intellectualistic. While it would probably be unfair to apply this epithet to Dewey's philosophy, it is nevertheless true that he sees philosophical problems as arising from social rather than intellectual sources. James regards them as fundamentally problems of morale. In "The Will To Believe" and in other essays he interprets a person's philosophical position as a source of self-confidence, in the absence of which he could not act.

McKeon goes on to explain and illustrate why philosophies employing different types of method cannot communicate with one another. We have already considered how a logistic method such as Husserl's would be opposed to a method of inquiry such as Dewey's. In particular, Dewey would regard Husserl's position as remote from the social milieu in which, in Dewey's view, philosophical problems occur and their solutions are tested (although he might admit that in an oblique way Husserl is attempting to conserve social values), while Husserl would surely see Dewey's philosophy as an attempt to socialize consciousness if not to naturalize it. Similar abysses separate dialectical methods from logistic methods on the one hand and from methods of inquiry on the other. On frequent occasions during his long career, Russell has attacked the dialectic of Hegel as illogical nonsense and as a philosophical endorsement of fascism. Dialectical philosophers for their part attack logistic philosophy on the ground that it is an empty formalism and a philosophical endorsement of anarchy or political naïveté. Philosophers of inquiry attack dialectical views because the larger whole through which such views attempt to reconcile all disagreements allegedly swallows up the concrete flesh-and-blood individual—it is, in a phrase that James used with approval "a lion's den to which all footsteps lead and from which none return." Dialectical philosophers impugn philosophies of inquiry as specimens of a shabby opportunism. McKeon concludes that "the relations among philosophies are not simple differences concerning the same or comparable problems." In fact "each method can claim the virtues of the other two while denying that the other methods in fact possess those virtues." Because of such differences, philosophical discussion can never come to an end. If one supposes that discussion has succeeded only when it has come to an end, McKeon's conclusion is that philosophical discussion is doomed to failure.

In point of fact, in the very act of starting the problem, McKeon has laid the groundwork for solving it. For the problem is a problem only from the dialectical point of view. Both logistic philosophies and philosophies of inquiry are committed to dismissing the radical oppositions of philosophies. Logistic philosophies will dismiss them as aberrations due to ignorance of the true goals of philosophy, and philosophies of inquiry will dismiss them as mere academic disputes. Only for dialectical philosophies is the existence of philosophical opposition itself a philosophical datum. If dialectical philosophies are concerned with reconciling radical disagreement, there seems no good reason why the disagreements of philosophers should necessarily fall beyond the scope of this concern. Obviously, since conflicting philosophies have different purposes and different methods, the "larger whole" in terms of which the reconciliation must be effected will have to be a totality of a fairly sophisticated kind. It must be of such a nature that the conflicting philosophies with their differing purposes and methods can still both acknowledge its existence. But there is nothing in the nature of the case impossible about this.

A step beyond the impasse described by McKeon is taken by R. G. Collingwood. Actually, all that Collingwood suggests, in effect, is that we look at the evidence McKeon has mustered in a slightly different light. One reason why McKeon's impasse seems so alarming is that we are given the impression that it has always existed and will always continue to exist in just its present form. But Collingwood intimates here (and asserts more emphatically in other writings) that different methods and purposes have come into prominence at different historical periods. The questions the Greek philosophers asked were not our questions. Although the English word "ought" is the closest we can come to translating the Greek word *dei,* this does not mean that the questions the Greeks asked about the nature of obligation were the same as the questions we ask about it. Hence their answers—their accounts of the nature of obligation—cannot be evaluated in the same light as our contemporary answers.

The apparent contradictions among widely differing philosophies, then, can be reconciled by seeing the philosophies not as competing recommendations of conflicting purposes and methods but as recommendations that do not compete because they are separated by intervals of historical time. The old does not compete with the new; each has its place in history. So historical time is seen as the "larger whole" in terms of which the dialectical reconciliation is effected. The view adumbrated here is close to Hegel's, which we outlined earlier.

Actually, Collingwood's argument is addressed not so much against the doubts of a McKeon as it is against a certain very common form of naïveté regarding the history of philosophy. This is the assumption that philosophers of different historical periods are trying to answer the same questions. Thus it is often supposed that Plato gave one set of answers and Thomas Hobbes (1588–1679) another to the same questions regarding the nature of man's political obligations—Plato in his *Republic* and Hobbes in his *Leviathan.*

If this were so, we should have to say that their answers were mutually inconsistent, and hence that not both sets of answers could be right." In general, philosophers often speak as follows of an author they are criticizing: "Our author is here trying to answer the following question. . . . That is a question which all philosophers ask themselves sooner or later; the right answer to it is. . . . Our author is giving one of the wrong answers." But Collingwood asserts that this sort of criticism is usually a fraud. When philosophers reach different conclusions, it is highly likely that they are answering different questions; and when they are, their answers cannot contradict one another, for "no two propositions can contradict one another unless they are answers to the same question."

It is often supposed, by philosophers as well as by laymen, that the problems of philosophy are eternal. The phrase *philosophia perennis* ("perennial philosophy") is used to denote the point of view from which the eternality of the problems is asserted and within which the attempt is continually made anew to grapple with them. Of the authors whose writings are included in this volume, Maritain especially represents the point of view of *philosophia perennis,* but Russell and Husserl also advocate it to some extent. Dewey and Cornforth, on the other hand, oppose it. Collingwood, for his part, vigorously attacks the assumption that there is a *philosophia perennis.* He introduces an explicitly historical dimension into the study of philosophy in such a way that problems lose their eternal status and become phenomena peculiar to their own historical periods. Collingwood makes an important contribution in *exposing* the assumption he attacks, even though we may not want to say that he conclusively *refutes* it.

The insight that we cannot hope to understand a philosophical doctrine unless we see what questions the doctrine is trying to answer is also expressed by Martin Heidegger, although with a different emphasis. According to Heidegger, in order to understand what philosophy is we must engage in "dialogue" with the great philosophers of the past. Such "dialogue" is more than imaginary conversation; it requires us actually to take the position of the past philosopher with whom we are concerned and to follow the path along which his philosophizing took him. We can do this only if we are properly "tuned" to the philosophical position we are trying to grasp.

Otherwise our understanding is only historical, not genuinely philosophical, and we have made no progress toward answering the question "What is philosophy?" in philosophical terms. Because he takes quite seriously the saying that the nature of philosophy is a philosophical question, Heidegger insists that to answer it in non-philosophical terms is not to answer it at all. And we succeed in answering it philosophically only when we are able to move along the path philosophy itself has taken.

Collingwood would presumably be satisfied that a person had understood a philosophical position if he could state the questions the position was intended to answer. But for Heidegger philosophical understanding requires much more than this. The mere ability to list the questions giving rise to a position might betoken a historical understanding of the position, but never a philosophical grasp of it. From Heidegger's point of view, Collingwood's approach is intellectualistic, presupposing, as it does, that the meaning of a philosophical position can always be puzzled out by a person intelligent enough to reconstruct the question from which the position arises. Conversely, Heidegger's approach is nonintellectualistic. When Heidegger speaks of "grasping" a philosophical position or the nature of philosophy, he is not referring to an intellectual achievement. To be "tuned" to a philosophy is not to have puzzled it out. It is rather to be dramatically identified with the position one grasps—to "stand in the shoes of" the philosopher whose position one is trying to understand.

The idea that there is a fundamental kind of knowledge or insight available only to those willing to "stand in someone else's shoes" has been widely proclaimed by many recent philosophers generally classified as existentialists, and Heidegger is regarded as one of the founders of existentialism. Precisely because of the nonintellectual nature of the kind of knowledge or insight it takes to be fundamental, existentialism has often been dismissed as an appeal to the emotions. How, after all, is a person to judge when he has succeeded in putting himself "in someone else's shoes" if he rejects intellectual means of judging? Apparently all that we can say of a person "tuned" to a philosophy is just that he has a grasp of the philosophy that is emotionally satisfying. Yet someone else, with a completely different grasp of the same position, might equally well be emotionally satisfied. If we forego the use of the intellect, who is to decide between them?

For Heidegger, however, it is clear that the emotions are not the criterion of correct "tuning." "Sentiments, even the finest," he says, "have no place in philosophy." The very contrast between intellect and emotions as possible channels through which we might become acquainted with philosophy presupposes a view of man's relation to philosophy that is, so far as Heidegger is concerned, profoundly wrong. When we think of intellect and the emotions as alternative ways of becoming acquainted with some object of concern—say a work of art or another person—we are presupposing that this object is something that we might not have become acquainted with at all. Whatever I could hope to get to know either through intellectual analysis or by emotional sympathy is something the existence of which is independent of my existence; I could perfectly well go on living without it. But for Heidegger, philosophy is indispensable to man's life. To exist as a man is to take a fundamental stand with respect to Being. This stand is essentially a questioning, so that man is essentially a being who questions the Being of all things ("the Being of being," in the translators' phrase), including his own Being. What does Heidegger mean by this "questioning"? One thing he means is "inquiry"—man is the being who inquires into the nature of Being, including the nature of his own Being. But he also means a certain fundamental anxiety man has with regard to Being. The very stand man takes in inquiring into the nature of Being seems to place him outside of Being and thus in danger of losing it. Both the inquiry and the anxiety are included in Heidegger's conception of philosophy. Philosophy is indispensable to human life because man must question Being in both of these ways.

We are in a position now to understand what Heidegger means in the selection included in this book when he says that man is "addressed" by Being and responds to it. "The answer to our question 'What is philosophy?' is not exhausted in an affirmation which answers to the question by determining what we are to understand by the concept 'philosophy.' The answer is not a reply . . . , the answer is rather the co-respondence[7] which responds to the Being

[7] The spelling of "co-respondence" here is that used by the translators of the selection used in this book.

of being." It is this co-respondence, or correspondence, to which Heidegger also refers as "tuning"; hence "tuning" is not an emotional response, but is rather the assumption of a basic philosophical stance in response to the question "What is philosophy?" Elsewhere—especially in his celebrated book *Being and Time*—Heidegger points out that while we are all addressed by Being, most of us conceal this fact from ourselves and evade our calling to undertake a philosophical quest.

Notice that Heidegger identifies the attitude we take when addressed by Being not only as questioning but also as wonder; and he reminds us that for the Greeks philosophy begins in wonder. Indeed, there is much in Heidegger's position that would have been acceptable to Plato, Aristotle, or even many medieval thinkers. The attitude toward Being to which Heidegger summons us is not unlike what the ancients called "wisdom." Heidegger himself has done much to support the contention that he is mainly proposing to return to an outlook of an earlier age.

We may seem to have come full circle. But to have traveled in a circle is not the same as to have been all the while standing still. Even if one were to take the extreme position that Heidegger's conception of philosophy coincides with the Greek conception, it could not be denied that in reaching this conception Heidegger considers and rejects other conceptions that have evolved over the long period that separates the Greeks from us, and which the Greeks themselves could not have seen as possible. We have seen what some of these conceptions are and how they are related to various conceptions of the goals and methods of philosophy. Even if we accept none of these views of the nature of philosophy, we may still learn something of its nature from an account of their variety and changeability.

JACQUES MARITAIN

The Nature of Philosophy and of Theology

Jacques Maritain (1882–   ) is a leader of the "Neo-Thomist" movement, which proposes a return to the philosophy of St. Thomas Aquinas especially insofar as this philosophy succeeds in harmonizing faith and reason. A native of France, Maritain studied philosophy at the Sorbonne under the great evolutionary thinker Bergson. Brought up as a Protestant, he was converted to Catholicism in 1906. After a long career as a writer and lecturer in France, Maritain came to the United States in 1940, and has taught at Columbia and Princeton Universities.

We shall take philosophy to mean philosophy *par excellence,* the first philosophy or *metaphysics.* What we shall say of it in the absolute sense . . . will be applicable relatively . . . to the other departments of philosophy.

Philosophy is not a "wisdom" of conduct or practical life that consists in acting well. It is a wisdom whose nature consists essentially in *knowing.*

How? Knowing in the fullest and strictest sense of the term, that is to say, *with certainty,* and in being able to state why a thing is what it is and cannot be otherwise, knowing *by causes.* The search for causes is indeed the chief business of philosophers, and the knowledge with which they are concerned is not a merely probable knowledge, such as orators impart by their speeches, but a knowledge which compels the assent of the intellect, like the knowledge which the geometrician conveys by his demonstrations. But certain knowledge of causes is termed *science.* Philosophy therefore is a science.

Knowing by what medium, by what light? Knowing by reason, by what is called the *natural light* of the human intellect. This is a quality common to every purely human science (as contrasted with

From *An Introduction to Philosophy* by Jacques Maritain, published by Sheed & Ward Inc., New York, pp. 102, 103–105, 107–110, 124–132, *passim.*

theology). That is to say, the rule of philosophy, its criterion of truth, is the evidence of its object. . . .

Knowing what? To answer this question we may recall the subjects which engaged the attention of the different philosophers whose teachings we have summarised. They inquired into everything—knowledge itself and its methods, being and non-being, good and evil, motion, the world, beings animate and inanimate, man and God. Philosophy therefore is concerned with everything, is a *universal* science.

This does not, however, mean that philosophy absorbs all the other sciences, or is the sole science, of which all the rest are merely departments; nor on the other hand that it is itself absorbed by the other sciences, being no more than their systematic arrangement. On the contrary, philosophy possesses its distinctive nature and object, in virtue of which it differs from the other sciences. If this were not the case philosophy would be a chimera. . . . But that philosophy is something real, and that its problems have the most urgent claim to be studied, is proved by the fact that the human mind is compelled by its very constitution to ask the questions which the philosophers discuss, questions which moreover involve the principles on which the certainty of the conclusions reached by every science in the last resort depends.

"You say," wrote Aristotle in a celebrated dilemma, "one must philosophise. Then you must philosophise. You say one should not philosophise. Then (to prove your contention) you must philosophise. In any case you must philosophise."

But how can philosophy be a *special* science if it deals with everything? We must now inquire under what aspect it is concerned with everything, or, to put it another way, what is that which in everything directly and for itself interests the philosopher. If, for example, philosophy studies man, its object is not to ascertain the number of his vertebrae or the causes of his diseases; that is the business of anatomy and medicine. Philosophy studies man to answer such questions as whether he possesses an intellect which sets him absolutely apart from the other animals, whether he possesses a soul, if he has been made to enjoy God or creatures, etc. When these questions are answered, thought can soar no higher. No problems lie beyond or above these. We may say then that the philosopher does not seek the explanation nearest to the phenomena perceived by our senses, but the explanation most remote from them, the ultimate explanation. This is expressed in philosophical terminology by saying that philosophy is not concerned with *secondary causes* or proximate explanations: [1] but on the contrary with *first causes*, highest principles or ultimate explanations.

Moreover, when we remember our conclusion that philosophy knows things by the natural light of reason, it is clear that it investigates the first causes or highest principles *in the natural order*. . . .

Thus philosophy, alone among the branches of human knowledge, has for its object everything which is. But in everything which is it investigates only the first causes. The other sciences, on the contrary, have for their object some particular province of being, of which they investigate only the secondary causes or proximate principles. That is to say, of all branches of human knowledge philosophy is the most sublime. . . .

The account we have just given is applicable in an unqualified sense only to the first philosophy or metaphysics, but may be extended to philosophy in general, if it is regarded as a body of which metaphysics is the head.[2] We shall then define philosophy in general as a universal body of sciences [3] whose . . . standpoint is first causes (whether absolutely first causes or principles, the formal object of metaphysics, or the first causes in a particular order, the . . . object of the other branches of philosophy). And it follows that metaphysics alone deserves the name of *wisdom*

[1] That is to say, approximating to the particulars of sensible phenomena.

[2] The ancients understood by the term *philosophy* the sum-total of the main branches of scientific study (*physics,* or the science of nature; *mathematics,* or the sciences of proportion; *metaphysics,* or the science of being as such; *logic;* and *ethics*). There could therefore be no question of distinguishing between philosophy and the sciences. The one question with which they were concerned was how to distinguish the first philosophy, or metaphysics, from the other sciences. We, on the contrary, since the enormous development of the special sciences, must distinguish from them not only metaphysics (the science of absolutely first principles) but the study of the first principles in a particular order (for instance, the mathematical or the physical); and the entire body of these constitutes what we call philosophy.

[3] Only metaphysics and logic constitute a universal science specifically one.

absolutely speaking . . . , the remaining branches of philosophy only relatively or from a particular point of view. . . .

> *Conclusion.* Philosophy is the science which by the natural light of reason studies the first causes or highest principles of all things—is, in other words, the science of things in their first causes, in so far as these belong to the natural order. . . .

We said above that philosophy is a science, and that it attains certain knowledge. By this we would not be understood to claim that philosophy provides certain solutions for *every* question that can be asked within its domain. On many points the philosopher must be content with probable solutions, either because the question goes beyond the actual scope of his science, for example in many sections of natural philosophy and psychology, or because of its nature it admits only of a probable answer, for example the application of moral rules to individual cases. But this element of mere probability is accidental to science as such. And philosophy yields a greater number of certain conclusions, and of those many more perfect, namely, the conclusions of metaphysics, than any other purely human science. . . .

Philosophy is the highest of the *human* sciences, that is, of the sciences which know things by the natural light of reason. But there is a science above it. For if there be a science which is a participation by man of the knowledge proper to God himself, obviously that science will be superior to the highest human science. Such a science, however, exists; it is *theology*.

The word *theology* means the science of God. The science or knowledge of God which we can attain naturally by the unassisted powers of reason, and which enables us to know God by means of creatures as the author of the natural order, is a philosophic science —the supreme department of metaphysics—and is known as *theodicy* or *natural theology.* The knowledge or science of God which is unattainable naturally by the unassisted powers of reason, and is possible only if God has informed men about himself by a revelation from which our reason, enlightened by faith, subsequently draws the implicit conclusions, is *supernatural theology* or simply *theology.* It is of this science that we are now speaking.

Its object is something wholly inaccessible to the natural apprehension of any creature whatsoever, namely, God known in himself, in his own divine life, . . . not, as in natural theology, God as the first cause of creatures and the author of the natural order. And all theological knowledge is knowledge in terms of God thus apprehended, whereas all metaphysical knowledge, including the metaphysical knowledge of God, is knowledge in terms of being in general.

The premisses of theology are the truths formally revealed by God (*dogmas* or articles of faith), and its primary criterion of truth the authority of God who reveals it.

Its light is no longer the more natural light of reason, but the light of reason illuminated by faith, *virtual revelation* in the language of theology, that is to say, revelation in so far as it implicitly (virtually) contains whatever conclusions reason can draw from it.

Alike by the sublimity of its object, the certainty of its premisses, and the excellence of its light, theology is above all merely human sciences. And although it is unable to perceive the truth of its premisses, which the theologian believes, whereas the premisses of philosophy are seen by the philosopher, it is nevertheless a science superior to philosophy. Though, as St. Thomas points out, the argument from authority is the weakest of all, where human authority is concerned, the argument from the authority of God, the revealer, is more solid and powerful than any other.

And finally as the object of theology is he who is above all causes, it claims with a far better title than metaphysics the name of *wisdom*. It is wisdom *par excellence*. What relations, then, must obtain between philosophy and theology?

As the superior science, theology *judges* philosophy in the same sense that philosophy judges the sciences. It therefore exercises in respect of the latter a function of guidance or government, though a negative government, which consists in rejecting as false any philosophic affirmation which contradicts a theological truth. In this sense theology controls and exercises jurisdiction over the conclusions maintained by philosophers.

The *premisses* of philosophy, however, are independent of theology, being those primary truths which are self-evident to the understanding, whereas the premisses of theology are the truths revealed by God. The premisses of philosophy are self-supported and are not derived from those of theology. Similarly the light by which philosophy knows its object is independent of theology, since its light is the light of *reason,* which is its own guarantee. For these reasons philosophy is not positively governed by theology, nor has it any need of theology to defend its premisses (whereas it defends those of the other sciences). It develops its principles autonomously within its own sphere, though subject to the external control and negative regulation of theology.

It is therefore plain that philosophy and theology are entirely distinct, and that it would be as absurd for a philosopher to invoke the authority of revelation to prove a philosophical thesis as for a geometrician to attempt to prove a theorem by the aid of physics, for example, by weighing the figures he is comparing. But if philosophy and theology are entirely distinct, they are not therefore unrelated, and although philosophy is of all the human sciences pre-eminently the free science, in the sense that it proceeds by means of premisses and laws which depend on no science superior to itself, its freedom—that is, its freedom to err—is limited in so far as it is subject to theology, which controls it externally.

In the seventeenth century the Cartesian reform resulted in the severance of philosophy from theology, the refusal to recognise the rightful control of theology and its function as a negative rule in respect of philosophy. This was tantamount to denying that theology is a science, or anything more than a mere practical discipline, and to claiming that philosophy, or human wisdom, is the absolutely sovereign science, which admits no other superior to itself. Thus, in spite of the religious beliefs of Descartes himself, Cartesianism introduced the principle of *rationalist* philosophy, which denies God the right to make known by revelation truths which exceed the natural scope of reason. For if God has indeed revealed truths of this kind, human reason enlightened by faith will inevitably employ them as premisses from which to obtain further knowledge and thus form a science, theology. And if theology is a science, it must exercise in respect of philosophy the function of a negative rule, since the same proposition cannot be true in philosophy, false in theology.

On the other hand, philosophy renders to theology services of the greatest value where it is employed by the latter. For in fact theology employs in its demonstrations truths proved by philosophy. Philosophy thus becomes the instrument of theology, and it is in this respect and in so far as it serves theological argument that it is called *ancilla theologiae*.[4] In itself, however, and when it is proving its own conclusions, it is not a bond-servant but free, subject only to the external control and negative ruling of theology.

As was shown above, philosophy is from the very nature of things obliged to employ as an instrument the evidence of the senses, and even, in a certain fashion, the conclusions of the special sciences. Theology, considered in itself as a science subordinate to the knowledge of God and the blessed, is not in this way obliged to make use of philosophy, but is absolutely independent.

In practice, however, on account of the nature of its possessor, that is to say, on account of the weakness of the human understanding, which can reason about the things of God only by analogy with creatures, it cannot be developed without the assistance of philosophy. But the theologian does not stand in the same relation to philosophy as the philosopher to the sciences. We have seen above that the philosopher should employ the propositions or conclusions which he borrows from the sciences, not to establish his own conclusions (at any rate not conclusions for which metaphysical certainty is claimed), but merely to illustrate his principles, and therefore that the truth of a metaphysical system does not depend on the truth of the scientific material it employs. The theologian, on the contrary, makes use at every turn of philosophic propositions to prove his own conclusions. Therefore a system of theology could not possibly be true if the metaphysics which it employed were false. It is indeed an absolute necessity that the theologian should have at his disposal a true philosophy in conformity with the common sense of mankind.

Philosophy taken in itself normally precedes theology. Certain fundamental truths of the natural order are indeed what we may term the introduction to the faith. . . . These truths, which are naturally known to all men by the light of common sense, are

[4] "The handmaid of theology."—Ed.

known and proved scientifically by philosophy. Theology, being the science of faith, presupposes the philosophical knowledge of these same truths.

Philosophy considered as the instrument of theology serves the latter, principally in three ways. In the first place theology employs philosophy to prove the truths which support the foundations of the faith in that department of theology which is termed apologetics which shows, for example, how miracles prove the divine mission of the Church; secondarily to impart some notion of the mysteries of faith by the aid of analogies drawn from creatures—as for instance when theology uses the philosophic conception of . . . the mental word to illustrate the dogma of the Trinity; and finally to refute the adversaries of the faith—as when theology shows by means of the philosophic theory of *quantity* that the mystery of the Eucharist is in no way opposed to reason.

We must not forget that, if philosophy serves theology, it receives in return valuable assistance from the latter.

In the first place, so far as it is of its nature subject to the external control and negative ruling of theology, it is protected from a host of errors; and if its freedom to err is thus restricted, its freedom to attain truth is correspondingly safeguarded.

In the second place, in so far as it is the instrument of theology, it is led to define more precisely and with more subtle refinements important concepts and theories which, left to itself, it would be in danger of neglecting.

Conclusion. Theology, or the science of God so far as He has been made known to us by revelation, is superior to philosophy. Philosophy is subject to it, neither in its premisses nor in its method, but in its conclusions, over which theology exercises a control, thereby constituting itself a negative rule of philosophy.

BERTRAND RUSSELL

On Scientific Method in Philosophy

Bertrand Arthur William Russell (1872–   ) is the grand old man of English philosophy. Author of more than fifty books including social tracts, historical studies, and detective stories as well as cardinally important contributions to symbolic logic and philosophy, Lord Russell has led a long, vigorous, and sometimes stormy career as a lecturer, conscientious objector (especially in World War I, when he was jailed for his views), free-thinker, advocate of free love, political iconoclast, and, most recently, "Ban the Bomb" marcher (again arrested). In 1950 he became the third philosopher ever to win the Nobel Prize for literature.

[In an earlier part of this essay Russell argues that a philosophy guided by scientific method cannot be concerned with the nature of the universe as a whole, or with the notion of *good and evil.*]

If the notion of the universe and the notion of good and evil are extruded from scientific philosophy, it may be asked what specific problems remain for the philosopher as opposed to the man of science? It would be difficult to give a precise answer to this question, but certain characteristics may be noted as distinguishing the province of philosophy from that of the special sciences.

In the first place a philosophical proposition must be general. It must not deal specially with things on the surface of the earth, or with the solar system, or with any other portion of space and time. It is this need of generality which has led to the belief that philosophy deals with the universe as a whole. I do not believe that this belief is justified, but I do believe that a philosophical proposition must be applicable to everything that exists or may exist. It might be supposed that this admission would be scarcely distinguishable from the view which I wish to reject. This, however, would be an error, and an important one. The traditional view would make the universe itself the subject of various predicates which could not

From Bertrand Russell, *Mysticism and Logic* (London: Allen & Unwin, 1929), pp. 110–114, 118–124. Used by permission of George Allen & Unwin Ltd.

be applied to any particular thing in the universe, and the ascription of such peculiar predicates to the universe would be the special business of philosophy. I maintain, on the contrary, that there are no propositions of which the "universe" is the subject; in other words, that there is no such thing as the "universe." What I do maintain is that there are general propositions which may be asserted of each individual thing, such as the propositions of logic. This does not involve that all the things there are form a whole which could be regarded as another thing and be made the subject of predicates. It involves only the assertion that there are properties which belong to each separate thing, not that there are properties belonging to the whole of things collectively. The philosophy which I wish to advocate may be called logical atomism or absolute pluralism, because, while maintaining that there are many things, it denies that there is a whole composed of those things. We shall see, therefore, that philosophical propositions, instead of being concerned with the whole of things collectively, are concerned with all things distributively; and not only must they be concerned with all things, but they must be concerned with such properties of all things as do not depend upon the accidental nature of the things that there happen to be, but are true of any possible world, independently of such facts as can only be discovered by our senses.

This brings us to a second characteristic of philosophical propositions, namely, that they must be *a priori*. A philosophical proposition must be such as can be neither proved nor disproved by empirical evidence. Too often we find in philosophical books arguments based upon the course of history, or the convolutions of the brain, or the eyes of shell-fish.[1] Special and accidental facts of this kind are irrelevant to philosophy, which must make only such assertions as would be equally true however the actual world were constituted.

We may sum up these two characteristics of philosophical propositions by saying that *philosophy is the science of the possible*. But this statement unexplained is liable to be misleading, since it may be thought that the possible is something other than the general, whereas in fact the two are indistinguishable.

Philosophy, if what has been said is correct, becomes indistinguishable from logic as that word has now come to be used. The

[1] Such arguments are commonly used to prove the existence of God.—Ed.

study of logic consists, broadly speaking, of two not very sharply distinguished portions. On the one hand it is concerned with those general statements which can be made concerning everything without mentioning any one thing or predicate or relation, such for example as "if x is a member of the class α and every member of α is a member of β, then x is a member of the class β, whatever x, α, and β may be." On the other hand, it is concerned with the analysis and enumeration of logical *forms*, i.e. with the kinds of propositions that may occur, with the various types of facts, and with the classification of the constituents of facts. In this way logic provides an inventory of possibilities, a repertory of abstractly tenable hypotheses.

It might be thought that such a study would be too vague and too general to be of any very great importance, and that, if its problems became at any point sufficiently definite, they would be merged in the problems of some special science. It appears, however, that this is not the case. In some problems, for example, the analysis of space and time, the nature of perception, or the theory of judgment, the discovery of the logical form of the facts involved is the hardest part of the work and the part whose performance has been most lacking hitherto. It is chiefly for want of the right logical hypothesis that such problems have hitherto been treated in such an unsatisfactory manner, and have given rise to those contradictions or antinomies in which the enemies of reason among philosophers have at all times delighted.

By concentrating attention upon the investigation of logical forms, it becomes possible at last for philosophy to deal with its problems piecemeal, and to obtain, as the sciences do, such partial and probably not wholly correct results as subsequent investigation can utilise even while it supplements and improves them. Most philosophies hitherto have been constructed all in one block, in such a way that, if they were not wholly correct, they were wholly incorrect, and could not be used as a basis for further investigations. It is chiefly owing to this fact that philosophy, unlike science, has hitherto been unprogressive, because each original philosopher has had to begin the work again from the beginning, without being able to accept anything definite from the work of his predecessors. A scientific philosophy such as I wish to recommend will be piecemeal and tentative like other sciences; above all, it will be able to invent hypotheses which, even if they are not wholly true, will yet remain fruitful after the necessary corrections have been made. This possibility of successive approximations to the truth is, more than anything else, the source of the triumphs of science, and to transfer this possibility to philosophy is to ensure a progress in method whose importance it would be almost impossible to exaggerate.

The essence of philosophy as thus conceived is analysis, not synthesis. To build up systems of the world, like Heine's German professor who knit together fragments of life and made an intelligible system out of them, is not, I believe, any more feasible than the discovery of the philosopher's stone. What is feasible is the understanding of general forms, and the division of traditional problems into a number of separate and less baffling questions. "Divide and conquer" is the maxim of success here as elsewhere.

Let us illustrate these somewhat general maxims by examining their application to the philosophy of space, for it is only in application that the meaning or importance of a method can be understood. Suppose we are confronted with the problem of space as presented in Kant's Transcendental Aesthetic,[2] and suppose we wish to discover what are the elements of the problem and what hope there is of obtaining a solution of them. It will soon appear that three entirely distinct problems, belonging to different studies, and requiring different methods for their solution, have been confusedly combined in the supposed single problem with which Kant is concerned. There is a problem of logic, a problem of physics, and a problem of theory of knowledge. Of these three, the problem of logic can be solved exactly and perfectly; the problem of physics

[2] The "Transcendental Aesthetic" is a section of Kant's *Critique of Pure Reason.* In this book Kant considers, among other things, the nature of geometry. Any geometrical truth, such as "A straight line is the shortest distance between two points," is regarded by Kant not only as a priori (see Russell's definition of this term on p. 38), but also as *synthetic,* in the sense that it does not strictly follow by the laws of logic from the definitions of the concepts it relates. "Being the shortest distance between two points," for example, is no part of the *meaning* of "straight line." In "The Transcendental Aesthetic" Kant explains how synthetic a priori truths are possible in geometry by asserting that such truths are simply consequences of an intuitive grasp of the nature of space that is shared by all men.—Ed.

can probably be solved with as great a degree of certainty and as great an approach to exactness as can be hoped in an empirical region; the problem of theory of knowledge, however, remains very obscure and very difficult to deal with. Let us see how these three problems arise.

[The "logical problem," according to Russell, is whether the theorems of geometry are true exclusively of some one kind of space. Pointing to non-Euclidean geometries, he concludes that space as an object of logical or mathematical study has lost its alleged uniqueness. On this basis, Russell also challenges Kant's claim that geometrical truths are synthetic (see footnote 2, p. 40), contending that "the nature of geometrical *reasoning* . . . is purely deductive and purely logical."

"The physical problem," says Russell, "may be stated as follows: to find in the physical world, or to construct from physical materials, a space of one of the kinds enumerated by the logical treatment of geometry." If we can solve this problem, it will follow that our knowledge of geometrical truths is not a priori. Russell briefly sketches a solution in which points and straight lines are defined in terms of physical entities.]

(3) The problem with which Kant is concerned in the Transcendental Aesthetic is primarily the epistemological problem: "How do we come to have knowledge of geometry *a priori?*" By the distinction between the logical and physical problems of geometry, the bearing and scope of this question are greatly altered. Our knowledge of pure geometry is *a priori* but is wholly logical. Our knowledge of physical geometry is synthetic, but is not *a priori.* Our knowledge of pure geometry is hypothetical, and does not enable us to assert, for example, that the axiom of parallels is true in the physical world. Our knowledge of physical geometry, while it does enable us to assert that this axiom is approximately verified, does not, owing to the inevitable inexactitude of observation, enable us to assert that it is verified *exactly*. Thus, with the separation which we have made between pure geometry and the geometry of physics, the Kantian problem collapses. To the question, "How is synthetic *a priori* knowledge possible?" we can now reply, at any rate so far

as geometry is concerned, "It is not possible," if "synthetic" means "not deducible from logic alone." Our knowledge of geometry, like the rest of our knowledge, is derived partly from logic, partly from sense, and the peculiar position which in Kant's day geometry appeared to occupy is seen now to be a delusion. There are still some philosophers, it is true, who maintain that our knowledge that the axiom of parallels, for example, is true of actual space, is not to be accounted for empirically, but is as Kant maintained derived from an *a priori* intuition. This position is not logically refutable, but I think it loses all plausibility as soon as we realise how complicated and derivative is the notion of physical space. As we have seen, the application of geometry to the physical world in no way demands that there should really be points and straight lines among physical entities. The principle of economy, therefore, demands that we should abstain from assuming the existence of points and straight lines. As soon, however, as we accept the view that points and straight lines are complicated constructions by means of classes of physical entities, the hypothesis that we have an *a priori* intuition enabling us to know what happens to straight lines when they are produced indefinitely becomes extremely strained and harsh; nor do I think that such an hypothesis would ever have arisen in the mind of a philosopher who had grasped the nature of physical space. . . .

Another question by which the capacity of the analytic method can be shown is the question of realism. Both those who advocate and those who combat realism seem to me to be far from clear as to the nature of the problem which they are discussing. If we ask: "Are our objects of perception *real* and are they *independent* of the percipient?" it must be supposed that we attach some meaning to the words "real" and "independent," and yet, if either side in the controversy of realism is asked to define these two words, their answer is pretty sure to embody confusions such as logical analysis will reveal.

Let us begin with the word "real." There certainly are objects of perception, and therefore, if the question whether these objects are real is to be a substantial question, there must be in the world two sorts of objects, namely, the real and the unreal, and yet the unreal is supposed to be essentially what there is not. The question what properties must belong to an object in order to make it real is one to which an adequate answer is seldom if ever forthcoming. There is of course the Hegelian answer, that the real is the self-consistent and that nothing is self-consistent except the Whole; but this answer, true or false, is not relevant in our present discussion, which moves on a lower plane and is concerned with the status of objects of perception among other objects of equal fragmentariness. Objects of perception are contrasted, in the discussions concerning realism, rather with psychical states on the one hand and matter on the other hand than with the all-inclusive whole of things. The question we have therefore to consider is the question as to what can be meant by assigning "reality" to some but not all of the entities that make up the world. Two elements, I think, make up what is felt rather than thought when the word "reality" is used in this sense. A thing is real if it persists at times when it is not perceived; or again, a thing is real when it is correlated with other things in a way which experience has led us to expect. It will be seen that reality in either of these senses is by no means necessary to a thing, and that in fact there might be a whole world in which nothing was real in either of these senses. It might turn out that the objects of perception failed of reality in one or both of these respects, without its being in any way deducible that they are not parts of the external world with which physics deals. Similar remarks will apply to the word "independent." Most of the associations of this word are bound up with ideas as to causation which it is not now possible to maintain. *A* is independent of *B* when *B* is not an indispensable part of the *cause* of A. But when it is recognised that causation is nothing more than correlation, and that there are correlations of simultaneity as well as of succession, it becomes evident that there is no uniqueness in a series of casual antecedents of a given event, but that, at any point where there is a correlation of simultaneity, we can pass from one line of antecedents to another in order to obtain a new series of causal antecedents. It will be necessary to specify the causal law according to which the antecedents are to be considered. I received a letter the other day from a correspondent who had been puzzled by various philosophical questions. After enumerating them he says: "These questions led me from Bonn to Strassburg, where I found Professor Simmel." Now, it would be absurd to deny that these questions caused his body to move from Bonn to Strassburg, and yet it must be supposed that a set of purely mechanical antecedents could also be found which would account for this transfer of matter from one place to another. Owing to this plurality of causal series antecedent to a given event, the notion of *the* cause becomes indefinite, and the question of independence becomes correspondingly ambiguous. Thus, instead of asking simply whether *A* is independent of *B*, we ought to ask whether there is a series determined by such and such causal laws leading from *B* to *A*. This point is important in connexion with the particular question of objects of perception. It may be that no objects quite like those which we perceive ever exist unperceived; in this case there will be a causal law according to which objects of perception are not independent of being perceived. But even if this be the case, it may nevertheless also happen that there are purely physical causal laws determining the occurrence of objects which are perceived by means of other objects which perhaps are not perceived. In that case, in regard to such causal laws objects of perception will be independent of being perceived. Thus the question whether objects of perception are independent of being perceived is, as it stands, indeterminate, and the answer will be yes or no according to the method adopted of making it determinate. I believe that this confusion has borne a very large part in prolonging the controversies on this subject, which might well have seemed capable of remaining for ever undecided. The view which I should wish to advocate is that objects of perception do not persist unchanged at times when they are not perceived, although probably objects more or less resembling them do exist at such times; that objects of perception are part, and the only empirically knowable part, of the actual subject-matter of physics, and are themselves properly to be called physical; that purely physical laws exist determining the character and duration of objects of perception without any reference to the fact that they are perceived; and that in the establishment of such laws the propositions of physics do not presuppose any propositions of psychology or even the existence of mind. I do not know whether realists would recognise such a view as realism. All that I should claim for it is, that it avoids difficulties which seem to me to beset both realism and idealism as hitherto advocated, and that it avoids the appeal which they have made to ideas which logical analysis shows to be ambiguous. A further defence and elaboration of the positions which I advocate, but for which time is lacking now, will be found indicated in my book on *Our Knowledge of the External World.*[3]

The adoption of scientific method in philosophy, if I am not mistaken, compels us to abandon the hope of solving many of the more ambitious and humanly interesting problems of traditional philosophy. Some of these it relegates, though with little expectation of a successful solution, to special sciences, others it shows to be such as our capacities are essentially incapable of solving. But there remain a large number of the recognised problems of philosophy in regard to which the method advocated gives all those advantages of division into distinct questions, of tentative, partial, and progressive advance, and of appeal to principles with which, independently of temperament, all competent students must agree. The failure of philosophy hitherto has been due in the main to haste and ambition: patience and modesty, here as in other sciences, will open the road to solid and durable progress.

[3] Open Court Company, 1914.

RUDOLF CARNAP

Philosophy and Logical Syntax

Rudolf Carnap (1891–) has made important contributions to mathematical logic as well as to philosophy. He received his Ph.D. degree from the University of Jena in 1921. As a university instructor in Vienna and later in Prague he helped to found the "Vienna Circle"—a group of scientists and philosophers who in the twenties and thirties developed the principles of logical positivism. Since coming to the United States in 1935, he has taught at the University of Chicago, Harvard, and the University of California at Los Angeles.

The questions dealt with in any theoretical field—and similarly the corresponding sentences and assertions—can be roughly divided into *object-questions* and *logical questions*. (This differentiation has no claim to exactitude; it only serves as a preliminary to the following non-formal and inexact discussion.) By object-questions are to be understood those that have to do with the objects of the domain under considerations, such as inquiries regarding their properties and relations. The logical questions, on the other hand, do not refer directly to the objects, but to sentences, terms, theories, and so on, which themselves refer to the objects. (Logical questions may be concerned either with the meaning and content of the sentences, terms, etc., or only with the form of these; of this we shall say more later.) In a certain sense, of course, logical questions are also object-questions, since they refer to certain objects—namely, to terms, sentences, and so on—that is to say, to objects of logic. When, however, we are talking of a non-logical, proper object-domain, the differentiation between object-questions and logical questions is quite clear. For instance, in the domain of zoology, the object-questions are concerned with the properties of animals, the relations of animals to one another and to other objects, etc.; the

From Rudolf Carnap, *The Logical Syntax of Language* (London: Routledge & Kegan Paul Ltd, 1937), pp. 277–280 and 284–285, used by permission of Routledge & Kegan Paul Ltd; and *Philosophy and Logical Syntax* (London: Kegan Paul, Trench, Trubner & Co., 1935), pp. 75–88, used by permission of the Orthological Institute, London.

logical questions, on the other hand, are concerned with the sentences of zoology and the logical connections between them, the logical character of the definitions occurring in that science, the logical character of the theories and hypotheses which may be, or have actually been, advanced, and so on.

According to traditional usage, the name 'philosophy' serves as a collective designation for inquiries of very different kinds. Object-questions as well as logical questions are to be found amongst these inquiries. The object-questions are in part concerned with supposititious objects which are not to be found in the object-domains of the sciences (for instance, the thing-in-itself, the absolute, the transcendental, the objective idea, the ultimate cause of the world, non-being, and such things as values, absolute norms, the categorical imperative, and so on); this is especially the case in that branch of philosophy usually known as metaphysics. On the other hand, the object-questions of philosophy are also concerned with things which likewise occur in the empirical sciences (such as mankind, society, language, history, economics, nature, space and time, causality, etc.); this is especially the case in those branches that are called natural philosophy, the philosophy of history, the philosophy of language, and so on. The logical questions occur principally in logic (including applied logic), and also in the so-called theory of knowledge (or epistemology), where they are, however, for the most part, entangled with psychological questions. The problems of the so-called philosophical foundations of the various sciences (such as physics, biology, psychology, and history) include both object-questions and logical questions.

The logical analysis of philosophical problems shows them to vary greatly in character. As regards those object-questions whose objects do not occur in the exact sciences, critical analysis has revealed that they are pseudo-problems. The supposititious sentences of metaphysics, of the philosophy of values, of ethics (in so far as it is treated as a normative discipline and not as a psychosociological investigation of facts) are pseudo-sentences; they have no logical content, but are only expressions of feeling which in their turn stimulate feelings and volitional tendencies on the part of the hearer. In the other departments of philosophy the psychological questions must first of all be eliminated; these belong to psychology, which is one of the empirical sciences, and are to be handled by it with the aid of its empirical methods. [By this, of course, no veto is put upon the discussion of psychological questions within the domain of logical investigation; everyone is at liberty to combine his questions in the way which seems to him most fruitful. It is only intended as a warning against the disregard of the difference between proper logical (or epistemological) questions and psychological ones. Very often the formulation of a question does not make it clear whether it is intended as a psychological or a logical one, and in this way a great deal of confusion arises.] The remaining questions, that is, in ordinary terminology, questions of logic, of the theory of knowledge (or epistemology), of natural philosophy, of the philosophy of history, etc., are sometimes designated by those who regard metaphysics as unscientific as questions of scientific philosophy. As usually formulated, these questions are in part logical questions, but in part also object-questions which refer to the objects of the special sciences. Philosophical questions, however, according to the view of philosophers, are supposed to examine such objects as are also investigated by the special sciences from quite a different standpoint, namely, from the purely philosophical one. As opposed to this, we shall here maintain that all these remaining philosophical questions are logical questions. Even the supposititious object-questions are logical questions in a misleading guise. The supposed peculiarly philosophical point of view from which the objects of science are to be investigated proves to be illusory, just as, previously, the supposed peculiarly philosophical realm of objects proper to metaphysics disappeared under analysis. Apart from the questions of the individual sciences, only the questions of the logical analysis of science, of its sentences, terms, concepts, theories, etc., are left as genuine scientific questions. We shall call this complex of questions the *logic of science*. . . .

According to this view, then, once philosophy is purified of all unscientific elements, only the logic of science remains. In the majority of philosophical investigations, however, a sharp division into scientific and unscientific elements is quite impossible. For this reason we prefer to say: *the logic of science takes the place of the inextricable tangle of problems which is known as philosophy*. Whether, on this view, it is desirable to apply the term 'philosophy' or 'scientific philosophy' to this remainder, is a question of expedience which cannot be decided here. It must be taken into consideration that the word 'philosophy' is already heavily burdened, and that it is largely applied (particularly in the German language) to speculative metaphysical discussions. The designation 'theory of knowledge' (or 'epistemology') is a more neutral one, but even this appears not to be quite unobjectionable, since it misleadingly suggests a resemblance between the problems of our logic of science and the problems of traditional epistemology; the latter, however, are always permeated by pseudo-concepts and pseudo-questions, and frequently in such a way that their disentanglement is impossible.

The view that, as soon as claims to scientific qualifications are made, all that remains of philosophy is the logic of science, cannot be established here and will not be assumed in what follows. In this part of the book we propose to examine the character of the sentences of the logic of science, and to show that they are syntactical sentences. For anyone who shares with us the antimetaphysical standpoint it will thereby be shown that all philosophical problems which have any meaning belong to syntax. The following investigations concerning the logic of science as syntax are not, however, dependent upon an adherence to this view; those who do not subscribe to it can formulate our results simply as a statement that the problems of that part of philosophy which is neither metaphysical nor concerned with values and norms are syntactical. . . .

We have already distinguished (in an inexact manner) between object-sentences and logical sentences. We will now contrast instead (at first also in an inexact manner) the two domains of *object-sentences* and *syntactical sentences,* only those logical sentences which are concerned with form being here taken into account and included in the second domain. Now there is an intermediate field between these two domains. To this intermediate field we will assign the sentences which are formulated as though they refer (either partially or exclusively) to objects, while in reality they refer to syntactical forms, and, specifically, to the forms of the designations of those objects with which they appear to deal. Thus these sentences are syntactical sentences in virtue of their content, though they are disguised as object-sentences. We will call them *pseudo-*

object-sentences. If we attempt to represent in a formal way the distinction which is here informally and inexactly indicated, we shall see that these pseudo-object-sentences are simply *quasi-syntactical sentences of the material mode of speech.* . . .

[I] propose to translate sentences which are formulated in the material mode of speech into the formal mode.[1] I do this for the purpose of showing that such sentences belong to the field of syntax. By the application of the material mode this character of the sentences is disguised; we are deceived—as we have seen—as to their real subject-matter. But there are still greater disadvantages of the material mode. It involves the danger of getting into useless philosophical controversies.

To take a case in point, in the different systems of modern arithmetic dealt with logically, numbers are given different status. For instance in the system of Whitehead and Russell numbers are treated as classes of classes,[2] while in the systems of Peano[3] and Hilbert[4] they are taken as primitive objects. Suppose two philosophers get into a dispute, one of them asserting: "Numbers are classes of classes," and the other: "No, numbers are primitive objects, independent elements." They may philosophize without end about the question what numbers really are, but in this way they will never come to an agreement. Now let them both translate their theses into the formal mode. Then the first philosopher makes the assertion: "Numerical expressions are class-expressions of the second order"; and the other says: "Numerical expressions are not class-expressions, but elementary expressions."

In this form, however, the two sentences are not yet quite complete. They are syntactical sentences concerning certain linguistic expressions. But a syntactical sentence must refer to one or several specific language-systems; it is incomplete unless it contains such a

[1] The formal mode of speech consists of syntactical sentences.—Ed.

[2] One of the purposes of *Principia Mathematica* (1910–1913) by Alfred North Whitehead and Bertrand Russell is to define the concept of number in terms of the allegedly simpler logical concept of class.—Ed.

[3] Giuseppe Peano (1858–1912) was a noted Italian pioneer in the foundations of mathematics.—Ed.

[4] David Hilbert (1862–1943) was a great German mathematician who investigated, among other things, the logical structure of mathematics.—Ed.

reference. If the language-system of Peano is called L_1, and that of Russell L_2, the two sentences may be completed as follows: "In L_1 numerical expressions are elementary expressions," and: "In L_2 numerical expressions are class expressions of the second order." Now these assertions are compatible with each other and both are true; the controversy has ceased to exist.

Very often sterile philosophical controversies arise through such an incompleteness of theses. This incompleteness is concealed by the usual formulation in the material mode. When translated into the formal mode, the want of reference to language is noticed at once. Then by adding such a reference the theses are made complete, and thereby the controversy becomes clear and exact. Even then it will sometimes still be difficult to decide which side is right; but sometimes it is as simple as in the example just considered, and the dispute obviously vanishes. *The relativity of all philosophical theses in regard to language*, that is, the need of reference to one or several particular language-systems, is a very essential point to keep in mind. It is on account of the general use of the material mode of speech that this relativity is nearly always left unnoticed.

PSEUDO-QUESTIONS

In the example mentioned the theses are only incomplete; they can easily be translated into the formal mode and completed, and thus they become precise. In other cases, however, the use of the material mode leads to metaphysical pseudo-theses which cannot be so easily corrected. I do not mean that the sentences of the material mode are themselves necessarily pseudo-theses or without sense, but only that they often mislead us into stating other sentences or questions which are so. For instance, in the material mode we speak about numbers instead of numerical expressions. That is not in itself bad or incorrect, but it leads us into the temptation to raise questions as to the real essence of numbers, such as the philosophical questions whether numbers are real objects or ideal objects, whether they are extramental or intramental, whether they are objects-in-themselves or merely intentional objects of thinking, and the like. I do not know how such questions could be translated into the formal mode or into any other unambiguous and clear mode; and I doubt whether the philosophers themselves who are dealing with them are able to give us any such precise formulation. Therefore it seems to me that these questions are metaphysical pseudo-questions.

If we use the formal mode of speech, we are not speaking about numbers, but about numerical expressions. We can then raise many questions concerning the syntactical character of the numerical expressions in a certain system or in different systems, but we do not arrive at pseudo-questions of the kind mentioned. Against these we are protected automatically, so to speak, by the use of the formal mode.

What are the practical consequences of these considerations as to the formulation of philosophical theses? There is no need to eliminate completely the material mode of speech. This mode is usual and perhaps sometimes suitable. But it must be handled with special caution. In all decisive points of discussion it is advisable to replace the material by the formal mode; and in using the formal mode, reference to the language-system must not be neglected. It is not necessary that the thesis should refer to a language-system already put forward; it may sometimes be desired to formulate a thesis on the basis of a so far unknown language-system, which is to be characterized by just this thesis. In such a case the thesis is not an assertion, but a proposal or project, in other words a part of the definition of the designed language-system.

If one partner in a philosophical discussion cannot or will not give a translation of his thesis into the formal mode, or if he will not state to which language-system his thesis refers, then the other will be well-advised to refuse the debate, because the thesis of his opponent is incomplete, and discussion would lead to nothing but empty wrangling.

One frequent cause of dispute amongst philosophers is the question what *things* really are. The representative of a Positivistic school asserts: "A thing is a complex of sense-data;" his Realistic adversary replies: "No, a thing is a complex of physical matter;" and an endless and futile argument is thus begun. Yet both are right after all; the controversy has arisen only on account of the unfortunate use of the material mode.

Let us translate the two theses into the formal mode. That of the Positivist becomes: "Every sentence containing a thing-designation is equipollent[5] with a class of sentences which contain no thing-designations, but sense-data-designations," which is true; the transformation into sense-data-sentences has often been shown in epistemology. That of the Realist takes the form: "Every sentence containing a thing-designation is equipollent with a sentence containing no thing-designation, but space-time-co-ordinates and physical functions," which is obviously also true.

In this case we do not even need to refer to two different language-systems in order to make the two theses compatible with one another. They are right in relation to our general language. Each of them asserts the possibility of a certain transformation of thing-sentences. As both kinds of transformation are found feasible, there is no inconsistency. In the original formulation in the material mode the theses *seemed* to be incompatible, because they *seemed* to concern the essence of things, both of them having the form: "A thing is such and such."

EPISTEMOLOGY

So far we have considered several examples of philosophical questions, and we have seen that we can translate these questions from the commonly used material mode of speech into the formal mode. By the possibility of this translation it is shown that they belong to syntax. Now the question arises whether the same consideration likewise applies to all other problems and theses of philosophy (where 'philosophy,' as explained before, is understood to include neither metaphysics nor psychology). It is my contention that it does. Let us glance at the principal parts of philosophy in order to examine this assertion.

Epistemology or theory of knowledge in its usual form contains both psychological and logical questions. The psychological questions here concern the procedure of knowledge, that is, the mental events by which we come to know something. If we surrender these questions to the psychologist for his empirical investigation, there remains the logical analysis of knowledge, or more precisely, the logical analysis of the examination and verification of assertions, because knowledge consists of positively verified assertions. Epis-

[5] Carnap calls two sentences "equipollent" when each of them implies the other.—Ed.

temological questions of this kind can certainly be expressed in the formal mode, because epistemological analysis, the question of the verification of a given sentence, has to refer—as we found in the first chapter—to those observation sentences which are deducible from the sentence in question. Thus the logical analysis of verification is the *syntactical* analysis of those transformation rules which determine the deduction of observation sentences. Hence *epistemology*—after elimination of its metaphysical and psychological elements—*is a part of syntax.*

NATURAL PHILOSOPHY

It may seem, perhaps, more important to give our attention to some of the special divisions of philosophy, than to discuss the general questions of epistemology. What is called *Natural Philosophy* is, in particular, attracting more and more interest at the present time. What is the subject-matter of this part of philosophy? Is its task the philosophical investigation of nature? The answer is, No; there can be no such thing as a philosophical investigation of nature, because whatever can be said about nature, that is about any events in time and space and about their connections, has to be said by the scientist on the basis of empirical investigation. There remains nothing for the philosopher to say in this field. Metaphysicians do, indeed, venture to make a lot of statements about nature, but such metaphysics is, as we have seen, not theory, but rather poetry. The object of scientifically treated natural philosophy is not nature, but the natural sciences, and its task is the logical analysis of science, in other words, the *syntactical* analysis of the language-system of science.

If in natural philosophy we deal, for instance, with the structure of space and time, then we are occupied in fact with the syntactical analysis of the rules which determine the formation or transformation of space- and time-expressions. The point may be clarified by considering the following thesis, which asserts one of the principal features of the space-time-structure: "Time is one-dimensional; space is three-dimensional." This sentence can be translated into the formal mode as follows: "A time-designation consists of one co-ordinate; a space-designation consists of three co-ordinates." In the same way the sentence "Time is infinite in both directions, namely that of the past and that of the future," can be translated into the sentence: "Any real-number-expression, positive or negative, without limit, can be taken as a time-co-ordinate." The question: "Has space a Euclidean or a non-Euclidean structure?" becomes, in the formal mode: "Are the syntactical rules according to which from certain distances others can be calculated, of the Euclidean type or of one of the non-Euclidean types?"

Thus all questions about the structure of space and time are *syntactical* questions, that is, questions about the structure of the language, and especially the structure of the formation and transformation rules concerning space- and time-co-ordinates.

In addition to the problems of space and time, contemporary natural philosophy is especially concerned with the problems of *causality*. These problems are syntactical problems concerning the syntactical structure of the system of physical laws, as for instance the question whether fundamental physical laws have the type of deterministic laws or that of merely statistical laws. This logical question is the core of the whole problem of Determinism, which is nearly always expressed in the material mode, and is in addition often mixed up with metaphysical pseudo-problems. Consequently its character as a syntactical problem has not been recognized.

The objection may perhaps be raised at this point that the form of physical laws depends upon the experimental results of physical investigations, and that it is not determined by a merely theoretical syntactical consideration. This assertion is quite right, but we must bear in mind the fact that the empirical results at which physicists arrive by way of their laboratory experiments by no means *dictate their choice* between the deterministic and the statistical form of laws. The form in which a law is to be stated has to be decided by an act of volition. This decision, it is true, depends upon the empirical results, but not logically, only practically. The results of the experiments show merely that one mode of formulation would be more suitable than another, that is, more suitable with regard to the whole system of physics. However close the practical connection between the empirical results and the form of physical laws may be, the question concerning the form of these laws is in every case a syntactical question, that is, a question which has to be formulated in syntactical terms.

It is, to be sure, a syntactical question concerning a language-system which has not yet been stated, but is still a matter of discussion. And in this discussion about the future form of physical language and especially the form of fundamental physical laws, physicists as well as logicians have to take part. A satisfactory solution can only be found if both points of view, the empirical view of physics and the formal one of syntax, are taken into consideration. This applies not only to the special problem of causality and determinism, but generally to all problems of natural philosophy, to all questions of the logical analysis of empirical science. All such questions are *syntactical* problems, but in their treatment the results of *empirical* investigation have also to be taken into consideration.

MAX BLACK

Linguistic Method in Philosophy

Max Black (1909–   ) was born in Russia and educated in England. Graduating from Cambridge with honors in mathematics, he took his Ph.D. degree in Mathematical Logic at London University. In 1940 he came to the United States to accept a professorship of philosophy at the University of Illinois. Later he became Sage Professor at Cornell. Black has served as visiting professor and lecturer all over the world, and is the author of many books on mathematics and philosophy.

In this essay I shall illustrate and explain a method having wide application to philosophical problems, especially to those connected with certain famous sceptical paradoxes. After centuries of discussion, philosophers are still embarrassed by the resurgence of doubts about free will, the reality of time, the existence of other minds and the external world, the possibility of knowledge about the future or matters of fact; and any method which promises to give a satisfactory and permanent answer to such sceptical questionings deserves careful examination. . . .

A characteristic soliloquy by a sceptic might take this form:

"We all know about color blindness; and experts tell us that adults who are color-blind very often escape detection. A man who is color-blind shows great skill in hiding his abnormality by noticing differences in texture, slight defects in material, and other minute details commonly overlooked. Therefore anybody—even my best friend—might be color-blind, for all I know. An expert psychologist might find out the truth by inventing artificial and complex situations. But even *his* tests might not serve, and a sufficiently ingenious man might still be able to conceal his abnormality. Why should there not be a type of color blindness too subtle for *any* psychologist ever to discover? A man *might* agree with other people's behavior in *every* respect and so elude *every* test that could be applied. How

From Max Black, *Language and Philosophy* (Ithaca: Cornell University Press, 1949), pp. 3, 12–22. Copyright, 1949, by Cornell University, used with permission of Cornell University Press.

could we ever know? Perhaps everybody is like this? And if I cannot be sure that my friend is not color blind, how can I be sure of *anything* about his experiences, or those of anybody else?"

From this point on, the argument takes a course with which we are . . . familiar: Since everybody might be color-blind in a way which no tests could reveal, it is impossible to be sure they are not. And exactly the same type of argument can of course be applied just as well to any other sense quality. We can never be sure that others do not smell when we see, or think when we feel, never be sure that they think or feel at all.

What has happened in the course of this imaginary, but quite characteristic, line of thought? The central point to emphasize is that the criteria of application of the term "color blindness" used by the speaker *have gradually shifted* in the course of the argument. At the outset, the color blindness to which reference is made was the kind studied by psychologists. This type of color blindness is important in certain practical contexts (say that of the selection of engine drivers) and is recognizable in such situations by the application of well-known tests. *This* kind of color blindness is *defined* in terms of capacity to satisfy the tests.

The claim that this type of color blindness is so defined does not imply that the term "color blindness" has a single, authoritative and explicit verbal definition. For some restricted purposes the term may be introduced into discourse by this kind of definition—a formal explanation of its meaning—but for ordinary purposes no precise statement of this kind is available. The claim that "color blindness," in the sense in which it is ordinarily used, is *defined* by its tests, does not assert that the tests are definite and precise. What is meant is that the use of the term is learned by taking note of the *kind* of thing which is evidence for that term's exemplification. We teach a child or a foreigner the *meaning* of the word "color blindness" by showing him situations in which the use of the term would be appropriate. We say, in effect, "this is a case of undoubted color blindness" and "that is a case of undoubted normality of color vision" and "that, again, is a borderline case." When the child or the foreigner has learned to describe these various situations as we do, we say he has learned to use the word. It would therefore be stupid o ask "Why should these vague tests be relevant to color blind-ness?"—just as stupid as asking "Why should pigs be called 'pigs'?" t is a *fact* that we do use the noise "pigs" to refer to porcine quad-upeds; it is a *fact* that the word "color blindness" is normally used o refer to a condition revealed by vaguely demarcated tests.

Nevertheless the sceptic is dissatisfied with the common usage of he vague term and would remain dissatisfied with every more recise substitute which the psychologist might invent. If we could ully understand the source of this dissatisfaction, we should be near o a solution of the sceptical paradoxes.

What worries the philosophical sceptic so much is that the ordi-nary tests of color blindness, from a certain standpoint, appear so *rbitrary*.

This arbitrariness can be made clear by thinking about cases of orderline successes in passing the tests. A man who passes the tests ow in vogue among psychologists might conceivably fail if the ests were made only *slightly* harder; and this hypothetical case oes not seem to differ *in principle* from that of a man, who, failing o pass the current tests, would be *called* "color-blind." The two ases are different, of course, for one man passes and the other fails he present tests of abnormality; but the difference seems so slight hat we can hardly help regarding it as unimportant. We feel a trong inclination (once we get into this way of thinking) to say hat the term "color blindness" *ought* to be applied also to the case f a man who would fail at the slightly harder level.

If the tests *are* slightly modified, however, in the way the sceptic vishes, exactly the same objections could be brought against the ew tests. And it is obvious that the same would be true of *every* efinition of "color blindness" by means of a finite number of tests. Jo matter *what* tests were proposed, we could always imagine a nan who just *barely managed* to pass them and always feel the ame inclination to say his case did not differ *in principle* from that f his more successful competitors.

We are thereby driven to use "color blindness" in what I shall call *limiting sense* (to be opposed to the *practical senses* of color blind-ness which are useful to the ordinary man or the psychologist). What especially characterizes the limiting sense of color blindness is he possibility of making such statements as that "there might be a

case of 'color blindness' (in this limiting sense) which *no* tests coul
reveal."[1]

Similarly a sceptic may say: "You cannot be sure of the resu
of tomorrow's elections, even if the Gallup Poll does give an ove
whelming majority for the Democrats. Even if all the voters tol
you their intentions in advance, you could not be sure, for the
might change their minds. Evidence about the future can never b
perfect."

Or he may say, following an ancient theological pattern: "A man
soul is clearly not the same as his body. He can lose both legs wit
out loss of consciousness, and the same might conceivably be tru
of the loss of any limb or bodily organ. Now imagine a man to los
the whole of his body. What is *then* left, what could not conceivabl
be felt or touched or communicated with, is what I call th
soul."

All three of these examples involve the introduction of limitin
senses of crucial terms. And to all of them one appropriate repl
would be "I fail to understand what you mean." If the sceptic use
"color blindness" initially in the way we commonly do (i.e., if w
understand him at the outset), he is talking about the kind of thin
revealed by *some* test however complicated. If he continues to mea
even a part of this, to talk of a color blindness which is *in principl*
not to be revealed is to contradict himself: it is to say that his limi
ing kind of color blindness both does and does not satisfy tests. An
if he means something different by "color blindness" *in his sens*
then all we can say is that we fail to understand either the denot
tion or the connotation of his term: his statements contain semanti
hiatuses.

Similar comment applies to the other two examples: *perfect* ev
dence for tomorrow's election results is a self-contradictory notio
if evidence still means what it usually means; but if it means som
thing else, the onus is upon the sceptic to explain what it *does* mea
The notion of an invisible man is intelligible, as is that of an odorle
and intangible man, but the notion of a soul with whom no con
munication could *in principle* be established is either self-contradi
tory or unintelligible. We can, by some stretch of the imaginatio
understand a Cheshire cat leaving only its grin behind; but a cat sar

[1] The meaning of "limiting sense" is explained later in this essay.

whiskers, sans body, sans grin, sans *everything*—everything that might somehow, sometime, be detected—is a mere nothing.

To drive home the futility of these linguistic proceedings, let us consider how a limiting sense of a term would be introduced into a language. We saw a little while ago how the meaning of the term "color blindness" (in its familiar practical use) is made plain to a child or foreigner. He is shown cases where the term does apply, cases where it does not apply, and cases where its application is "doubtful" or "indeterminate." And it was a very important part of this learning procedure that cases of applicability were *contrasted* with cases of nonapplicability. We learn what "color blindness" means by getting to know what would be evidence for its *presence* and what would be evidence for its *absence*. Exactly the same is true of all terms applying to items or aspects of experience. We learn to use the word "knowledge" by contrasting cases of knowledge with cases of doubt and knowledge to the contrary; we learn to use "red" by learning the difference between cases of things being colored red, and their being colored green or some other color; we understand the word "variable" when we can distinguish a symbol which is a variable from one which is a constant, and so on.

Now suppose that, after a child had learned to use a term in this familiar way, the sceptic were to try to introduce to him a *limiting* sense of the term. Obviously the sceptic cannot produce *specimens:* for it is part of his contention that no specimens of the applications of terms in *his* senses can ever be encountered; the best he can do is to say something like this: "You have learned that there is a whole series of harder and harder tests of color blindness and corresponding *degrees* of that abnormality. Now imagine a color blindness *just like the kind with which you are already familiar,* but satisfying *none* of this series of tests—a color blindness infinitely hard to detect."

Or he says "You know what is meant by saying that this evidence for the result of tomorrow's election is stronger than that; you know how to arrange evidence about the character of the future in a series of steadily increasing probability. Now imagine evidence *just like the kind you already know* but so strong that its probability could not be increased—infinitely probable evidence. That is what I call *real* evidence about the future."

Or he says, "Imagine a man to lose his body; what remains unaffected by injury, death, or decay is what I call the real, the essential man."

If we try to obey such linguistic instructions as these, we are bound to get into insuperable difficulties. It is as if we were told that a physical object were not really small unless it did not exist at all; or that an egg was not really cooked until it was boiled an infinite length of time. The new instructions in the limiting use of the terms conflict with the older explanations for the practical use of the homonyms.

It should, by now, be clear why a limiting sense of color blindness (or any other term) could never be explained or conveyed to another person. Yet it is just such limiting senses that the sceptic needs if he is to have anything of philosophical importance to say. For any practical doubt about the determination of color blindness in the practical sense could be resolved by practical procedures. (The sceptic is not concerned with the uncertainty of stock markets, the efficiency of psychometrists, or the difficulty of being in the right place to observe an eclipse.)

The label of "*limiting* sense" has been deliberately used to suggest an analogy with the process of "proceeding to the limit" which occurs in mathematics. It is of course a mathematical commonplace that assertions which are true of every member of a converging sequence of quantities may cease to hold where limiting values are inserted. (Thus every member of an infinite sequence may be greater than zero while the limiting value of the sequence is *equal* to zero.) And mathematicians are constantly on guard against the dangers of extrapolating their definitions to apply to limiting cases.

A simple mathematical example of the illegitimate introduction of limiting senses would arise if we were to talk about the *terminal digit of an infinite decimal.*

To talk in this way is to *assume* that the new phrase has denotation, and in this instance the assumption is unjustified. Every finite (or terminating) decimal has of course a final digit. But to ask the value of *the* terminal digit of an infinite decimal is to do one of two things: *either* to imply that an infinite decimal has a final digit (a self-contradiction) *or* to introduce a *new but undefined and unexplained* locution.

It may be objected that the extrapolation of meanings is a procedure very characteristic of mathematics and the empirical sciences. And so it is; the history of mathematics and empirical science is full of fumbling attempts to introduce new terms. But these historical instances (of the first introduction of such terms as "infinitesimal," "infinite sum," "irrational number," "potential energy," "quasi-species," and the like) differ in an important respect from the philosophical transformations of common language. The mathematician or scientist introduces new terms to permit him to describe newly discovered relationships (homologous to those already in his possession). The first descriptions introduced may be confused and Pickwickian distortions of older terms, *but the new technical terms eventually receive an intelligible and self-consistent definition.*

The sceptic's attempt to introduce new terms is different. *He* has made no startling or unexpected discoveries about other minds, the future, or the external world; he is no fine connoisseur of evidence, prognostication, or moral judgment. He knows just what any other man knows, but insists on describing that knowledge differently. His alteration of common language is pointless because it serves no purpose at all except that of confusion of thought.

I have been trying to hold distinct two different ways in which pointless alteration of language can happen. When a term is used in a limiting sense in such a way that part of the original meaning is retained, it is *self-contradictory;* when continuity with the original meaning is severed, so that no clue is left to the intended meaning of the term in its new usage, it may be said to be used *vacuously.* Our criticism of the sceptical argument can now be summarized by saying that it involves the use of crucial terms in senses which are either vacuous or self-contradictory.

It has been urged that the philosopher is driven into the extremes of irrefutable scepticism by a search for distinctions *of principle* arising from dissatisfaction with the vagueness and continuity of application of ordinary language. The sceptic does succeed in the end in making a distinction of principle; but the principle is that involved in the distinction between a term having some meaning, though vague and fluctuating, and another incapable of exemplification because it is vacuous or self-contradictory by definition. The presence of such terms renders the sceptical objections in a very important respects meaningless. . . .

All the examples so far used illustrate transition to limiting vacuity or self-contradiction. In other cases where linguistic considerations of the type which I have been presenting are relevant, a different though related pattern of thought may be observed.

This may be shown by considering one plausible retort to the above arguments against scepticism with respect to the existence of other minds. The sceptic might well object to the accusation that his use of "color blindness" or the more inclusive term "experience" is vacuous. For, he might say, *he himself* has actual experience of sense qualities, an experience *not identical* with its outward manifestations. Since "experience" means, for him, something *over and above* the tests, the term is *not* vacuous.

With part of this objection there is no need to disagree. It may be granted that a pain is not the *same* as its manifestations. But since the assertion has a deceptive appearance of being empirical it might be better to rephrase it in some such form as "we do not mean by 'pain' the same as 'manifestations of pain'; the 'manifestations' are symptoms of or evidence *for* the pain; they are not identical with the pain."

But though this is granted, the conclusion desired by the sceptic does not follow. And here again the procedure recommended is a careful consideration of how the sceptic could explain or introduce that sense of experience in which it refers to something accessible to him alone.

Once again we should begin by considering carefully how we learn to understand and above all to *contrast* such phrases as "*my* experience," "*your* experience," and "*his* experience" in practical contexts. There are familiar and common usages of these related expressions, and to understand them is to know the empirical tests which would be relevant to their exemplification. About these terms, in their familiar uses in practical contexts, there is no mystery and no *philosophical* problem.

Next we imagine the sceptic trying to explain what he means by an experience accessible to him alone. We may perhaps suppose him to be making an empirical assertion—implying perhaps that he himself is maladroit in speech and gestures. No, we are told, the difficulty is not of that practical order at all. Indeed, he assures us (for we remember that he is committed to the extremities of scepticism), this experience of which he speaks has *no* connection with its outward manifestations. Indeed it is a kind of accident that his experiences are accompanied by those outward symptoms. In some other possible world, he might have laughed where he now cries; in still another, feelings, even the strongest, might never be displayed at all. Nothing that we see or hear or touch is evidence *at all* for the personal and "private" sense qualities he is designating.

If he does say all this, we ought to reply that we *literally fail to understand what he means.* He doesn't mean what we *normally* mean by another person's experience, for the character of such experience we *can* infer from observations. But what else he means has not been made clear; the term "private experience" (experience in principle inaccessible to observation) is vacuous.

This case differs from that of "color blindness" (discussed earlier) in the absence of any progression to the limit. The root of the trouble in this and some other versions of solipsism or idealism seems to be in the determination to apply a term *universally*, so that *every* item of knowledge shall be called a case of *my* knowledge or experience.

The explanations so far given are unlikely to convince a *genuine* sceptic; for he still has many lines of defense. He might perhaps retort that it is *we* who are stretching the common and familiar use of the term "meaning"; that he himself very well understands what he is talking about; that we must have understood him or else have had nothing to which to object; and that it is absurd to suggest that a man like Hume might have talked nonsense without knowing it!

Our response to this counterattack will be the same as that already sufficiently illustrated. We must try to get our sceptic to reflect upon the ways in which he now uses "meaning," to consider the tests he would be prepared to accept as constitutive of its application, and especially to examine the ways in which his tests differ from those already current.

The linguistic analysis is here more difficult in proportion to the notorious ambiguity of the central term "meaning." And we must not suppose that the simple critical considerations previously presented will serve without modification. The prevalence of linguistic confusions of the type I have been discussing is evidence of the difficulty of the critical enterprise here recommended. A full examination of the puzzles connected with solipsism alone would demand thorough discussion of a whole group of cross-related terms (especially the epistemological ones, "possibility," "knowledge," and so on).

Experience in the criticism of such puzzles suggests that the sceptical difficulty does in many cases arise from the surreptitious introduction of vacuous or self-contradictory terminology. Where the cases differ is in the great variety of routes by which competent and determined thinkers are led into making such terminological changes.

The method here recommended would be effective to the degree that it was able to take account of such individual differences. To say "it is all a matter of words" is too easy to be rewarding. What should be done is to show in detail exactly what it is that makes such formulas as "Everything is really mind," or "A proposition is nothing but its method of verification," or "Truth is only practical usefulness," or "Ethical judgments are mere exclamations" so perennially attractive (though not to all philosophers at once).

At some point in these wider explorations, we could make good use of a general description of those features of language which are of special relevance to philosophical puzzles.

The last point to be made concerns the *type* of evidence which could be produced in defense of the procedures here recommended. All that needs to be said at present is that the evidence is no more esoteric or otherwise mysterious than that employed in any empirical enterprise. We are, it is true, not offering direct evidence for or against the sceptic's position (except in a preliminary stage of the proceedings). But we do invite him to reflect conscientiously and persistently upon the meanings of the terms he is using. Evidence for the meaning of terms is obtained by the makers of dictionaries in perfectly familiar ways; the case of individual and variant or fluctuating meanings is more difficult of resolution, but the difficulty is a *practical* one. When we are engaged in clarifying genuine philosophical difficulties, the author of the paradox may be the best judge of the success with which his linguistic and epistemological intentions are made plain to him. But the methods he uses in detecting his own meanings are the ordinary empirical ones which can in principle be employed by any lexicographer, or translator, or linguist.

Philosophical clarification of meaning is, on this view, as practical as slum clearance and as empirical as medicine.

MAURICE CORNFORTH

The Task of Philosophy

Maurice Cornforth (1909–) was born in London. After receiving first class honors in philosophy from both London University and Cambridge University, he became District Organizer of the Communist Party for the Eastern Counties of England. Since 1945 he has been associated with the British Communist press. He is the author of a number of books expounding Marxist doctrines.

Positivism rules out from philosophy all consideration of the nature of the objective world, and similarly of the thought processes through which we build our knowledge of the objective world. It succeeds only in reducing philosophy to a barren, abstract and formal analysis of language.

But philosophy is the attempt to understand the nature of the world and our place and destiny in it. The task of philosophers has always been to enrich this understanding and to generalise its conclusions. This is what the great systematic philosophers of the past essentially tried to do. And the measure of their greatness has always been the extent to which they succeeded in expressing in their philosophical generalisations the totality of social experience and scientific discovery available at their time. This explains, incidentally, why it is always impossible either to appreciate or criticise them except on the basis of a consideration of the historical circumstances which at once conditioned the way their problems were presented and the way they set about solving them.

The positivists, and particularly the latest "logical" positivists, explicitly reject the classical aim of philosophy to give an account of the world and of man. They reject philosophy because they separate it from science and from life. They begin by saying that whatever we can know about the world and about human society is expressed in the propositions of the natural and social sciences, and that phi-

From Maurice Cornforth, *Science Versus Idealism* (New York: International Publishers Co., Inc., 1962), pp. 219–223, 242–244. Used by permission of International Publishers and Lawrence & Wishart Ltd, London.

losophy has nothing to do with either—it is concerned with analysis of language, a particular, specialised study. Then from this analysis of language they go on to say that the sciences can reveal nothing about the objective world—about the objective laws of motion and interconnection in nature and society—but are concerned solely with the correlation of observational data. Thus their rejection of philosophy in the classical sense is at the same time a rejection of scientific knowledge. When they reject philosophy as an account of the nature of the world and of human society, they are at the same time rejecting science.

In opposition to positivism, it is necessary to reinstate the classical aim of philosophy. But not in the sense of inventing new philosophical systems. Their time is indeed past. There can no longer be room for any philosophy standing above the sciences and claiming to base a universal system of the world on principles different from those employed in empirical scientific investigation.

What is required of philosophy is rather that it should draw its principles and conclusions from the sciences themselves; that it should be a generalisation of the sciences, based on the sciences and continually enriched as the sciences advance; and that it should at the same time itself become a weapon of the sciences, a method penetrating the sciences and guiding the strategy of scientific research and the formulation of scientific theory.

And in contrast to the systems of the past, whose aim was confined to interpreting the world, such a philosophy has the aim of showing how men can effectively change the world.

In the course of its gigantic development in modern times, the scientific method of investigation has been extended to cover field after field, so that no part, no aspect of nature or of human society is closed to scientific investigation. There have been scored major achievements of scientific analysis—the analysis of complexes into their constituents, of macro-processes into micro-processes. And from this development of science in its entirety has emerged the conclusion that neither the world as a whole nor any of its parts can be regarded, as both scientists and philosophers tended to regard it in the 17th and 18th centuries, as something whose general nature was fixed and static—given once and for all; but that the world as a whole and everything in it is subject to the laws of change and takes part in a historical process of development.

From the static conception of nature as the eternal repetition of the same kinds of processes, in which the same kinds of things keep on repeating the same kinds of movement, science has advanced to evolutionary conceptions. Evolutionary ideas have taken possession of one field after another—for instance, in the theories of the origin and development of the solar system, and likewise of the stars and of the galaxy; in geology, which traces the history of the evolution of the earth's crust; in another way in chemistry, with Mendeleyev's periodic scheme of the elements; in biology, with the theory of the evolution of organic species; and in the various conceptions of the stage-by-stage evolution of human society.

From all this, then, stands out a fundamental task of philosophy, which is to generalise from the sciences the conception of the laws of change and development manifested in nature and society; and in discovering these most general laws—the laws of dialectics—to provide the sciences with a theoretical instrument, a method, for the prosecution of their researches and for the theoretical formulation of the laws of motion operative in their particular spheres.

Again, the advance to evolutionary conceptions in science, which expressed the discovery of the real evolution in nature and society, coincided with the developing of industrial capitalism in the late 18th century and in the 19th century. But this coincidence was no mere coincidence: it expressed a causal connection. The rise of industrial capitalism and of the industrial bourgeoisie, which supplanted the earlier manufacturing and mercantile phase, not only set science new problems to answer and directed inquiry into new fields, arising from the transformation taking place in all spheres of production; it bred the conception that in human society and throughout the whole of nature nothing was permanent and fixed, but everything was in process of change—that a continual forward movement was the law of the universe.

This meant that in every sphere science looked for, and found, not fixity but process.

"The bourgeoisie," wrote Marx and Engels, "cannot exist without constantly revolutionising the instruments of production, and thereby the relations of production, and with them the whole relations of society. Conservation of the old modes of production in unaltered form was, on the contrary, the first condition of existence for all earlier industrial classes. Constant revolutionising of production, uninterrupted disturbance of all social conditions, everlasting uncertainty and agitation, distinguish the bourgeois epoch from all earlier ones. All fixed, fast frozen relations, with their train of ancient and venerable prejudices and opinions, are swept away, all new-formed ones become antiquated before they can ossify." [1]

These were the conditions which gave rise to the conception of a universal evolution in nature and society. And thus the task of philosophy, to generalise the laws of change and development, follows, not only from the discoveries of the sciences, but from the whole complex of the movement of modern society in its entirety.

But more than that. This problem of philosophy is no mere academic problem of generalisation, but takes on a peculiar practical urgency.

The bourgeoisie has continually revolutionised the instruments of production, and enormous new powers of production are placed at the disposal of society. But capitalist society is rent with contradictions. While production has become socialised, it is still subjected to private, capitalist appropriation.

"In this contradiction, which gives the new mode of production its capitalist character, the whole conflict of today is already present in germ," wrote Engels. "The more the new mode of production gained the ascendancy in all decisive fields of production and in all countries of decisive economic importance, pressing back individual production into insignificant areas, the more glaring necessarily became the incompatibility of social production and capitalist appropriation. . . . The contradiction between social production and capitalist appropriation became manifest as the antagonism between the proletariat and the bourgeoisie . . ." and again as "the antagonism between the organisation of production in the individual factory and the anarchy of production in society as a whole. The capitalist mode of production moves in these two forms of the contradiction immanent in it from its very nature." [2]

[1] Marx and Engels: *Manifesto of the Communist Party,* ch. I.

[2] Engels: *Socialism, Utopian and Scientific,* ch. 3.

It results that men in capitalist society face a contrast between the enormous new powers of production at their disposal and their apparent lack of ability to control and organise them. Instead of leading to universal plenty, the growth of the powers of production leads to recurrent economic crises, to unemployment, to poverty and to war.

This means that the philosophical problem of generalising the laws of change and development becomes the problem of so understanding the forces at work in the processes in which we ourselves are involved that we are able to master them. The problem of finding how to interpret the world becomes the problem of finding how to change it. Philosophy must cease to be only the intellectual exercise of men learning and must become the possession of the masses, their theoretical weapon in their struggle to end the conditions which oppress them and to find the road to emancipation. . . .

PHILOSOPHERS AS THE PRODUCTS OF THEIR TIMES

Philosophy, of course, is an instance of the social division of labour. Out of the general division of intellectual and manual labour emerge various divisions of specialised thinkers, amongst them the individuals with an urge to philosophy. Thus the production of philosophy is a very different process from the production of myths and primitive ways of thinking. . . . Philosophy is the work of individual philosophers—highly specialised people, highly gifted people and intensely individual people. And the reflection of the economic basis takes place through the medium of their individual, personal thought.

It will be found, however, that in every epoch the ways of thinking characteristic of the philosophers do reflect the character of the economic development and production relations of that epoch. With all their intellectual labour after truth the philosophers cannot free themselves from the actual material circumstances under which they live.

For example, Marx and Engels wrote that "the bourgeoisie, wherever it has got the upper hand, has put an end to all feudal, patriarchal, idyllic relations. It has pitilessly torn asunder the motley feudal ties that bound man to his 'natural superiors,' and has left no other nexus between man and man than naked self-interest, than callous 'cash payment.' "[3]

It is impossible not to recognise the reflection of this state of affairs in bourgeois philosophy from its very inception—and not merely the acceptance of this state of affairs and the assertion of ideas corresponding to it in opposition to feudal ideas, but also the recognition of the problems that arise from it and the attempt to grapple with and solve those problems.

And this reflection is to be found not only in the realm of social philosophy. For example, it was typical of the natural philosophy or physics of the feudal period that insistence was continually laid on final causes. Everything was regarded as having its proper place in the universe and its end which it subserved. Thus bodies were said to fall because that was their proper motion. The earth was in the centre, and the proper place of earthy bodies was in the centre, towards which they naturally tended. The natural motion of fire, on the other hand, was upwards. And just as the bourgeoisie in its economic activity set about destroying the feudal relations which were reflected in these feudal ideas (and that reflection, too, by the way, was complicated and indirect: the feudal ideologists proceeded by adapting much earlier Greek ideas, and in particular the philosophy of Aristotle, for their own purposes); so the bourgeois philosophers and scientists proceeded by destroying—and they did so quite consciously—these feudal ideas. By doing so they made a mighty advance in science and philosophy, a truly revolutionary advance, just as capitalism was a revolutionary advance on feudalism. But their own outlook was by no means a product of pure thought or of pure intellectual criticism, but was itself determined, formed and bounded by the new social relations within which the philosophers were confined.

[3] Marx and Engels: *Manifesto of the Communist Party*, ch. I.

JOHN DEWEY

Changing Conceptions of Philosophy

John Dewey (1859–1952) is often said to have been the greatest American philosopher, and it is widely held that the "Instrumentalism" he advocated is the most important philosophical doctrine to have originated in the United States. Dewey was born in Vermont. After receiving his Ph.D. at the University of Michigan, he taught there for ten years before moving to the University of Chicago. There he pursued his growing interests in primary education and founded an experimental school where the highly influential methods of "Progressive Education" were developed. At Columbia University from 1904 until 1930 Dewey concentrated on philosophy, and wrote his most important books on Instrumentalism. He applied its principles to ethics, politics, aesthetics, metaphysics, and logic, as well as to education. In addition to being an author, Dewey was an experienced and perceptive traveler whose opinions were widely sought abroad.

We need to recognize that the ordinary consciousness of the ordinary man left to himself is a creature of desires rather than of intellectual study, inquiry or speculation. Man ceases to be primarily actuated by hopes and fears, loves and hates, only when he is subjected to a discipline which is foreign to human nature, which is, from the standpoint of natural man, artificial. Naturally our books, our scientific and philosophical books, are written by men who have subjected themselves in a superior degree to intellectual discipline and culture. Their thoughts are habitually reasonable. They have learned to check their fancies by facts, and to organize their ideas logically rather than emotionally and dramatically. When they do indulge in reverie and day-dreaming—which is probably more of the time than is conventionally acknowledged—they are aware of what they are doing. They label these excursions, and do not confuse their results with objective experiences. We tend to judge others by ourselves, and because scientific and philosophic books are composed by men in whom the reasonably, logical and

From John Dewey, *Reconstruction in Philosophy* (Enlarged edition; Boston: Beacon Press, 1948), Chap. I. Used by permission of the Beacon Press.

objective habit of mind predominates, a similar rationality has been attributed by them to the average and ordinary man. It is then overlooked that both rationality and irrationality are largely irrelevant and episodical in undisciplined human nature; that men are governed by memory rather than by thought, and that memory is not a remembering of actual facts, but is association, suggestion, dramatic fancy. The standard used to measure the value of the suggestions that spring up in the mind is not congruity with fact but emotional congeniality. Do they stimulate and reinforce feeling, and fit into the dramatic tale? Are they consonant with the prevailing mood, and can they be rendered into the traditional hopes and fears of the community? If we are willing to take the word dreams with a certain liberality, it is hardly too much to say that man, save in his occasional times of actual work and struggle, lives in a world of dreams, rather than of facts, and a world of dreams that is organized about desires whose success and frustration form its stuff.

To treat the early beliefs and traditions of mankind as if they were attempts at scientific explanation of the world, only erroneous and absurd attempts, is thus to be guilty of a great mistake. The material out of which philosophy finally emerges is irrelevant to science and to explanation. It is figurative, symbolic of fears and hopes, made of imaginations and suggestions, not significant of a world of objective fact intellectually confronted. It is poetry and drama, rather than science, and is apart from scientific truth and falsity, rationality or absurdity of fact in the same way in which poetry is independent of these things.

This original material has, however, to pass through at least two stages before it becomes philosophy proper. One is the stage in which stories and legends and their accompanying dramatizations are consolidated. At first the emotionalized records of experiences are largely casual and transitory. Events that excite the emotions of an individual are seized upon and lived over in tale and pantomime. But some experiences are so frequent and recurrent that they concern the group as a whole. They are socially generalized. The piecemeal adventure of the single individual is built out till it becomes representative and typical of the emotional life of the tribe. Certain incidents affect the weal and woe of the group in its entirety and thereby get an exceptional emphasis and elevation. A certain texture of tradition is built up; the story becomes a social heritage and possession; the pantomime develops into the stated rite. Tradition thus formed becomes a kind of norm to which individual fancy and suggestion conform. An abiding framework of imagination is constructed. A communal way of conceiving life grows up into which individuals are inducted by education. Both unconsciously and by definite social requirement individual memories are assimilated to group memory or tradition, and individual fancies are accommodated to the body of beliefs characteristic of a community. Poetry becomes fixated and systematized. The story becomes a social norm. The original drama which re-enacts an emotionally important experience is institutionalized into a cult. Suggestions previously free are hardened into doctrines. . . .

Although a necessary antecedent, this organization and generalization of ideas and principles of belief is not the sole and sufficient generator of philosophy. There is still lacking the motive for logical system and intellectual proof. This we may suppose to be furnished by the need of reconciling the moral rules and ideals embodied in the traditional code with the matter of fact positivistic knowledge which gradually grows up. For man can never be wholly the creature of suggestion and fancy. The requirements of continued existence make indispensable some attention to the actual facts of the world. Although it is surprising how little check the environment actually puts upon the formation of ideas, since no notions are too absurd not to have been accepted by some people, yet the environment does enforce a certain minimum of correctness under penalty of extinction. That certain things are foods, that they are to be found in certain places, that water drowns, fire burns, that sharp points penetrate and cut, that heavy things fall unless supported, that there is a certain regularity in the changes of day and night and the alternation of hot and cold, wet and dry:—such prosaic facts force themselves upon even primitive attention. Some of them are so obvious and so important that they have next to no fanciful context. Auguste Comte[1] says somewhere that he knows of no savage people who had a God of weight although every other natural quality or force may have been deified. Gradually there grows

[1] French philosopher and founder of positivism (1798–1857).—Ed.

up a body of homely generalizations preserving and transmitting the wisdom of the race about the observed facts and sequences of nature. This knowledge is especially connected with industries, arts and crafts where observation of materials and processes is required for successful action, and where action is so continuous and regular that spasmodic magic will not suffice. Extravagantly fantastic notions are eliminated because they are brought into juxtaposition with what actually happens. . . .

. . . The time came when matter of fact knowledge increased to such bulk and scope that it came into conflict with not merely the detail but with the spirit and temper of traditional and imaginative beliefs. Without going into the vexed question of how and why, there is no doubt that this is just what happened in what we term the sophistic movement in Greece, within which originated philosophy proper in the sense in which the western world understands that term. The fact that the sophists had a bad name given them by Plato and Aristotle, a name they have never been able to shake off, is evidence that with the sophists the strife between the two types of belief was the emphatic thing, and that the conflict had a disconcerting effect upon the traditional system of religious beliefs and the moral code of conduct bound up with it. Although Socrates was doubtless sincerely interested in the reconciliation of the two sides, yet the fact that he approached the matter from the side of matter of fact method, giving its canons and criteria primacy, was enough to bring him to the condemnation of death as a contemner of the gods and a corrupter of youth.

The fate of Socrates and the ill-fame of the sophists may be used to suggest some of the striking contrasts between traditional emotionalized belief on one hand and prosaic matter of fact knowledge on the other:—the purpose of the comparison being to bring out the point that while all the advantages of what we call science were on the side of the latter, the advantages of social esteem and authority, and of intimate contact with what gives life its deeper lying values were on the side of traditional belief. To all appearances, the specific and verified knowledge of the environment had only a limited and technical scope. It had to do with the arts, and the purpose and good of the artisan after all did not extend very far. They were subordinate and almost servile. Who would put the art of the shoemaker on the same plane as the art of ruling the state? Who would put even the higher art of the physician in healing the body, upon the level of the art of the priest in healing the soul? Thus Plato constantly draws the contrast in his dialogues. The shoemaker is a judge of a good pair of shoes, but he is no judge at all of the more important question whether and when it is good to wear shoes; the physician is a good judge of health, but whether it is a good thing or not to be well or better to die, he knows not. While the artisan is expert as long as purely limited technical questions arise, he is helpless when it comes to the only really important questions, the moral questions as to values. Consequently, his type of knowledge is inherently inferior and needs to be controlled by a higher kind of knowledge which will reveal ultimate ends and purposes, and thus put and keep technical and mechanical knowledge in its proper place. Moreover, in Plato's pages we find, because of Plato's adequate dramatic sense, a lively depicting of the impact in particular men of the conflict between tradition and the new claims of purely intellectual knowledge. The conservative is shocked beyond measure at the idea of teaching the military art by abstract rules, by science. One does not just fight, one fights for one's country. Abstract science cannot convey love and loyalty, nor can it be a substitute, even upon the more technical side, for those ways and means of fighting in which devotion to the country has been traditionally embodied. . . .

Yet the more acute and active minds, like that of Plato himself, could no longer be content to accept, along with the conservative citizen of the time, the old beliefs in the old way. The growth of positive knowledge and of the critical, inquiring spirit undermined these in their old form. The advantages in definiteness, in accuracy, in verifiability were all on the side of the new knowledge. Tradition was noble in aim and scope, but uncertain in foundation. The unquestioned life, said Socrates, was not one fit to be lived by man, who is a questioning being because he is a rational being. Hence he must search out the reason of things, and not accept them from custom and political authority. What was to be done? Develop a method of rational investigation and proof which should place the essential elements of traditional belief upon an unshakable basis; develop a method of thought and knowledge which while purifying tradition should preserve its moral and social values unimpaired; nay, by purifying them, add to their power and authority. To put it in a word, that which had rested upon custom was to be restored, resting no longer upon the habits of the past, but upon the very metaphysics of Being and the Universe. Metaphysics is a substitute for custom as the source and guarantor of higher moral and social values—that is the leading theme of the classic philosophy of Europe, as evolved by Plato and Aristotle—a philosophy, let us always recall, renewed and restated by the Christian philosophy of Medieval Europe.

Out of this situation emerged, if I mistake not, the entire tradition regarding the function and office of philosophy which till very recently has controlled the systematic and constructive philosophies of the western world. If I am right in my main thesis that the origin of philosophy lay in an attempt to reconcile the two different types of mental product, then the key is in our hands as to the main traits of subsequent philosophy so far as that was not of a negative and heterodox kind. In the first place, philosophy did not develop in an unbiased way from an open and unprejudiced origin. It had its task cut out for it from the start. It had a mission to perform, and it was sworn in advance to that mission. It had to extract the essential moral kernel out of the threatened traditional beliefs of the past. So far so good; the work was critical and in the interests of the only true conservatism—that which will conserve and not waste the values wrought out by humanity. But it was also precommitted to extracting this moral essence in a spirit congenial to the spirit of past beliefs. The association with imagination and with social authority was too intimate to be deeply disturbed. It was not possible to conceive of the content of social institutions in any form radically different from that in which they had existed in the past. It became the work of philosophy to justify on rational grounds the spirit, though not the form, of accepted beliefs and traditional customs.

The resulting philosophy seemed radical enough and even dangerous to the average Athenian because of the difference of form and method. In the sense of pruning away excrescences and eliminating factors which to the average citizen were all one with the basic beliefs, it was radical. But looked at in the perspective of history and in contrast with different types of thought which developed later in different social environments, it is now easy to see how profoundly, after all, Plato and Aristotle reflected the meaning of Greek tradition and habit, so that their writings remain, with the writings of the great dramatists, the best introduction of a student into the innermost ideals and aspirations of distinctively Greek life. Without Greek religion, Greek art, Greek civic life, their philosophy would have been impossible; while the effect of that science upon which the philosophers most prided themselves turns out to have been superficial and negligible. This apologetic spirit of philosophy is even more apparent when Medieval Christianity about the twelfth century sought for a systematic rational presentation of itself and made use of classic philosophy, especially that of Aristotle, to justify itself to reason. A not unsimilar occurrence characterizes the chief philosophic systems of Germany in the early nineteenth century, when Hegel assumed the task of justifying in the name of rational idealism the doctrines and institutions which were menaced by the new spirit of science and popular government. The result has been that the great systems have not been free from party spirit exercised in behalf of preconceived beliefs. Since they have at the same time professed complete intellectual independence and rationality, the result has been too often to impart to philosophy an element of insincerity, all the more insidious because wholly unconscious on the part of those who sustained philosophy.

And this brings us to a second trait of philosophy springing from its origin. Since it aimed at a rational justification of things that had been previously accepted because of their emotional congeniality and social prestige, it had to make much of the apparatus of reason and proof. Because of the lack of intrinsic rationality in the matters with which it dealt, it leaned over backward, so to speak, in parade of logical form. In dealing with matters of fact, simpler and rougher ways of demonstration may be resorted to. It is enough, so to say, to produce the fact in question and point to it—the fundamental form of all demonstration. But when it comes to convincing men of the truth of doctrines which are no longer to be accepted upon the say-so of custom and social authority, but which also are not capable of empirical verification, there is no recourse save to magnify the signs of rigorous thought and rigid demonstration. Thus arises that appearance of abstract definition and ultra-scientific argumentation which repels so many from philosophy but which has been one of its chief attractions to its devotees.

At the worst, this has reduced philosophy to a show of elaborate terminology, a hair-splitting logic, and a fictitious devotion to the mere external forms of comprehensive and minute demonstration. Even at the best, it has tended to produce an overdeveloped attachment to system for its own sake, and an over-pretentious claim to certainty. Bishop Butler declared that probability is the guide of life; but few philosophers have been courageous enough to avow that philosophy can be satisfied with anything that is merely probable. The customs dictated by tradition and desire had claimed finality and immutability. They had claimed to give certain and unvarying laws of conduct. Very early in its history philosophy made pretension to a similar conclusiveness, and something of this temper has clung to classic philosophies ever since. They have insisted that they were more scientific than the sciences—that, indeed, philosophy was necessary because after all the special sciences fail in attaining final and complete truth. There have been a few dissenters who have ventured to assert, as did William James, that "philosophy is vision" and that its chief function is to free men's minds from bias and prejudices and to enlarge their perceptions of the world about them. But in the main philosophy has set up much more ambitious pretensions.

To say frankly that philosophy can proffer nothing but hypotheses, and that these hypotheses are of value only as they render men's minds more sensitive to life about them, would seem like a negation of philosophy itself.

In the third place, the body of beliefs dictated by desire and imagination and developed under the influence of communal authority into an authoritative tradition, was pervasive and comprehensive. It was, so to speak, omnipresent in all the details of the group life. Its pressure was unremitting and its influence universal. It was then probably inevitable that the rival principle, reflective thought, should aim at a similar universality and comprehensiveness. It would be as inclusive and far-reaching metaphysically as tradition had been socially. Now there was just one way in which this pretension could be accomplished in conjunction with a claim of complete logical system and certainty.

All philosophies of the classic type have made a fixed and fundamental distinction between two realms of existence. One of these corresponds to the religious and supernatural world of popular tradition, which in its metaphysical rendering became the world of highest and ultimate reality. Since the final source and sanction of all important truths and rules of conduct in community life had been found in superior and unquestioned religious beliefs, so the absolute and supreme reality of philosophy afforded the only sure guaranty of truth about empirical matters, and the sole rational guide to proper social institutions and individual behavior. Over against this absolute and noumenal reality which could be apprehended only by the systematic discipline of philosophy itself stood the ordinary empirical, relatively real, phenomenal world of everyday experience. It was with this world that the practical affairs and utilities of men were connected. It was to this imperfect and perishing world that matter of fact, positivistic science referred.

This is the trait which, in my opinion, has affected most deeply the classic notion about the nature of philosophy. Philosophy has arrogated to itself the office of demonstrating the existence of a transcendent, absolute or inner reality and of revealing to man the nature and features of this ultimate and higher reality. It has therefore claimed that it was in possession of a higher organ of knowledge than is employed by positive science and ordinary practical experience, and that it is marked by a superior dignity and importance—a claim which is undeniable *if* philosophy leads man to proof and intuition of a Reality beyond that open to day-by-day life and the special sciences.

This claim has, of course, been denied by various philosophers from time to time. But for the most part these denials have been agnostic and sceptical. They have contented themselves with asserting that absolute and ultimate reality is beyond human ken. But they have not ventured to deny that such Reality would be the appropriate sphere for the exercise of philosophic knowledge provided only it were within the reach of human intelligence. Only comparatively recently has another conception of the proper office of philosophy arisen. . . . At this point, it can be referred to only by anticipation and in cursory fashion. It is implied in the account which has been given of the origin of philosophy out of the background of an authoritative tradition; a tradition originally dictated by man's imagination working under the influence of love and hate and in the interest of emotional excitement and satisfaction. Common frankness requires that it be stated that this account of the origin of philosophies claiming to deal with absolute Being in a systematic way has been given with malice prepense. It seems to me that this genetic method of approach is a more effective way of undermining this type of philosophic theorizing than any attempt at logical refutation could be.

If this lecture succeeds in leaving in your minds as a reasonable hypothesis the idea that philosophy originated not out of intellectual material, but out of social and emotional material, it will also succeed in leaving with you a changed attitude toward traditional philosophies. They will be viewed from a new angle and placed in a new light. New questions about them will be aroused and new standards for judging them will be suggested.

If any one will commence without mental reservations to study the history of philosophy not as an isolated thing but as a chapter in the development of civilization and culture; if one will connect the story of philosophy with a study of anthropology, primitive life, the history of religion, literature and social institutions, it is confidently asserted that he will reach his own independent judgment as to the worth of the account which has been presented today. Considered in this way, the history of philosophy will take on a new significance. What is lost from the standpoint of would-be science is regained from the standpoint of humanity. Instead of the disputes of rivals about the nature of reality, we have the scene of human clash of social purpose and aspirations. Instead of impossible attempts to transcend experience, we have the significant record of the efforts of men to formulate the things of experience to which they are most deeply and passionately attached. Instead of impersonal and purely speculative endeavors to contemplate as remote beholders the nature of absolute things-in-themselves, we have a living picture of the choice of thoughtful men about what they would have life to be, and to what ends they would have men shape their intelligent activities.

Any of you who arrives at such a view of past philosophy will of necessity be led to entertain a quite definite conception of the scope and aim of future philosophizing. He will inevitably be committed to the notion that what philosophy has been unconsciously, without knowing or intending it, and, so to speak, under cover, it must henceforth be openly and deliberately. When it is acknowledged that under disguise of dealing with ultimate reality, philosophy ha been occupied with the precious values embedded in social traditions, that it has sprung from a clash of social ends and from a conflict of inherited institutions with incompatible contemporary tendencies, it will be seen that the task of future philosophy is to clarify men's ideas as to the social and moral strifes of their own day. Its aim is to become so far as is humanly possible an organ for dealing with these conflicts. That which may be pretentiously unreal when it is formulated in metaphysical distinctions becomes intensely significant when connected with the drama of the struggle of social beliefs and ideals. Philosophy which surrenders its somewhat barren monopoly of dealings with Ultimate and Absolute Reality will find a compensation in enlightening the moral forces which move mankind and in contributing to the aspirations of men to attain to a more ordered and intelligent happiness.

EDMUND HUSSERL

Philosophy as a Strict Science

Edmund Husserl (1859–1938), whose contributions to the phenomenological movement in contemporary European philosophy were perhaps the most influential, received his Ph.D. in mathematics from the University of Vienna. Certain questions about the foundations of mathematics led him to become interested in philosophy, which he then taught at the German universities of Halle, Göttingen, and, finally, Freiburg-im-Breisgau. Although he published relatively little in his lifetime, he left behind thousands of pages of notes which reveal an indefatigable preoccupation with philosophical fundamentals.

[Husserl begins by asserting that although philosophy has always claimed to be a strict science, it has never lived up to this claim.]

I do not say that philosophy is an imperfect science; I say simply that it is not yet a science at all, as science it has not yet begun. As a criterion for this take any portion however small of theoretical content which has been objectively grounded. All sciences are imperfect, even the much-admired exact sciences. On the one hand they are incomplete, because the limitless horizon of open problems, which will never let the drive toward knowledge rest, lies before them; and on the other hand they have many lacunae in their already developed subject-matter, there remain evidences here and there of a lack of clarity or perfection in the systematic ordering of proofs and theories. Nevertheless, they do have a subject-matter, which is constantly growing and branching out in new directions. No reasonable person will doubt the objective truth, or at least the objectively grounded probability of the wonderful theories of mathematics and the natural sciences. Here there is, by and large, no room for private "opinions," "notions," or "points of view." To the extent that there are such in particular instances, the science in question

From *Philosophy as a Strict Science*, by Edmund Husserl and translated by Quentin Lauer, to be published in Torchbook series by Harper & Row, Publishers, Incorporated. Used by permission of Harper & Row.

is not established as such but is in the process of becoming a science, and is in general so judged.

The imperfection of philosophy is of an entirely different sort from that of the other sciences as just described. It is in possession not merely of an incomplete and, in particular, imperfect system of doctrine, but of none whatever. Each and every question is herein controverted, every position is matter of individual conviction, of the interpretation given by a school, of a "point of view." . . .

The following arguments are based on the conviction that the highest interests of human culture demand the development of a rigorously scientific philosophy; consequently, if a philosophical revolution in our times is to be justified, it must without fail be animated by the purpose of laying a new foundation for philosophy in the sense of strict science. This purpose is by no means foreign to the present age. It is fully alive precisely in the naturalism which dominates the age. From the start naturalism sets out with a firm determination to realize the ideal of a rigorously scientific reform of philosophy. It even believes at all times, both in its earlier and in its modern forms, that it has already realized this idea. But all this takes place, when we look at it from the standpoint of principle, in a form which from the ground up is replete with erroneous theory; and this, from a practical point of view means a growing danger for our culture. It is important today to engage in a radical criticism of naturalistic philosophy. In particular there is need of a positive criticism of principles and methods, as opposed to a purely negative criticism based on consequences. Only such a criticism is calculated to preserve intact confidence in the possibility of a scientific philosophy, a confidence which is threatened by the absurd consequences of a naturalism built on strict empirical science. . . .

NATURALISTIC PHILOSOPHY

Naturalism is a phenomenon consequent upon the discovery of nature, which is to say of nature considered as a unity of spatio-temporal being subject to exact laws of nature. With the gradual realization of this idea in constantly new natural sciences, which guarantee strict knowledge regarding many matters, naturalism proceeds to expand more and more. . . .

Characteristic of all forms of extreme and consistent naturalism, from popular naturalism to the most recent forms of sensation-monism and energism, is on one hand the *naturalizing of consciousness,* including all intentionally immanent data of consciousness, and on the other the *naturalizing of ideas* and consequently of all ideals and norms. . . .

[HOW PSYCHOLOGY HAS "NATURALIZED CONSCIOUSNESS"]

All natural science is naive in regard to its point of departure. The nature which it will investigate is for it simply there. Of course *there are* things, as things at rest, in motion, changing in unlimited space, and temporal things in unlimited time. We perceive them, we describe them by means of simple empirical judgments. It is the aim of natural science to know these self-evident data in an objectively valid, strictly scientific manner. The like is true in regard to nature in the broader, psychophysical sense, or in regard to the sciences which investigate it, in particular, therefore, in regard to psychology. The psychical does not constitute a world for itself; it is given as an ego or as the experience of an ego (by the way, in a very different sense), and this sort of thing reveals itself empirically as bound to certain physical things called bodies. This, too, is a self-evident pre-datum.

It is the task of psychology to investigate scientifically this psychical element in the psycho-physical makeup of nature, to determine it in an objectively valid way, to discover the laws according to which it develops and changes, comes into being and disappears. Every psychological determination is by that very fact psychophysical, which is to say in the broadest sense (which we retain from now on), that it has a never-failing physical connotation. Even where psychology—the empirical science—is oriented toward the determination of mere events of consciousness and not toward those which depend on the psychophysical in the ordinary narrower sense, still these events are thought of as those of nature, i.e. as belonging to human or animal consciousness, which for their part have a self-evident connection with human and animal bodies, along with which they are grasped. To eliminate the relation to nature would deprive the psychical of its character as an objectively-temporally determinable fact of nature, in short, of its character as a psychological fact. Let us, then, hold fast to this: every psychological judgment involves the existential positing of physical nature, whether expressly or not. . . .

How can experience as consciousness give or contact an object? How can experiences be mutually legitimated or corrected by means of each other, and not merely replace each other or confirm each other subjectively? How can the play of a consciousness whose logic is empirical make objectively valid statements, valid for things which are in and for themselves? Why are the playing rules, so to speak, of consciousness not irrelevant for things? How is natural science to be comprehensible in absolutely every case, to the extent that it pretends at every step to posit and to know a nature which is in itself—in itself in opposition to the subjective flow of consciousness? All these questions become riddles, as soon as reflexion on them becomes serious. It is well known that [theory of knowledge] is the discipline which wants to answer such questions, and that up to the present, despite all the thoughtfulness which the greatest scholars have employed in their regard, has not answered in a manner scientifically clear, unanimous, and decisive.

It requires only rigorous consistency in maintaining the level of this problematic (a consistency which, it is true, has been missing in *all* theories of knowledge up to the present) to see clearly the *absurdity* of a theory of knowledge based on natural science, and thus too of any psychological theory of knowledge. If certain riddles are, generally speaking, in principle inherent in natural science, then it is self-evident that the solution of these riddles according to premises and conclusions in principle transcends natural science. To expect from natural science itself the solution of any one of the problems which are inherent in it *as such*—thus inhering through and through, from beginning to end—or even merely to suppose that it could contribute to the solution of such a problem any *premises* whatever, is to be involved in a vicious circle. . . .

[PHENOMENOLOGY AS OPPOSED TO "A NATURAL SCIENCE ABOUT CONSCIOUSNESS"]

What it means, that objectivity *is* and manifests itself cognitively as so being, must precisely become evident purely from consciousness itself, and thereby it must become completely understandable. And for that is required a study of the *entire* consciousness, since according to *all* its forms it enters into possible cognitive functions. To the extent, however, that every consciousness is "consciousness-of," the essential study of consciousness includes also that of consciousness-meaning and consciousness-objectivity as such. To study any kind of objectivity whatever according to its general essence (a study which can pursue interests far removed from those of [theory of knowledge] and the investigation of consciousness) means to concern oneself with objectivity's modes of givenness and to exhaust its essential content in the processes of "clarification" proper to it. Even if the orientation is not that which is directed toward the kinds of consciousness and to an essential investigation of them, still the method of clarification is such that even here reflexion on the modes of being intended and of being given cannot be avoided. In any case, however, the clarification of all fundamental kinds of objectivities is for its part indispensable for the essential analysis of consciousness and as a result is included in it; primarily, however, in an epistemological analysis, which finds its task precisely in the investigation of correlations. Consequently we include all such studies, even though relatively they are to be distinguished, under the title *phenomenological.*

With this we meet a science—of whose extraordinary extent our contemporaries have as yet no concept—which, it is true, is a science of consciousness and still not psychology, a *phenomenology of consciousness,* as opposed to a *natural science about consciousness.* Since, however, there will be no question here of an accidental equivocation, it is to be expected beforehand that phenomenology and psychology must stand in close relationship to each other, in so far as both are concerned with consciousness, even though in a different way, according to a different "orientation." What we should like to express thereby is that psychology is concerned with "empirical consciousness," with consciousness from the empirical point of view, as an empirical being in the ensemble of nature; whereas phenomenology is concerned with "pure" consciousness, i.e. consciousness from the phenomenological point of view.

If this is correct, the result would then be—without taking away from the truth that psychology no more is nor can be philosophy than natural science can—that for essential reasons psychology must be more closely related to philosophy (i.e. through the medium of phenomenology) and must in its destiny remain most intimately bound up with philosophy. It would, finally, be possible to foresee that any psychologistic theory of knowledge must owe its existence to the fact that, missing the proper sense of the epistemological problematic, it is a victim of a presumably facile confusion between pure and empirical consciousness. To put the same in another way: it "naturalizes" pure consciousness.

This is in fact my interpretation, and it should in what follows be illustrated somewhat more clearly. . . .

Does . . . a psychology have a claim to "exactness," which leaves the concepts which *determine* its objects without scientific fixation, without methodical elaboration? No more, obviously, than would a physics which would be satisfied with the everyday concepts of heavy, warm, mass, etc. Modern psychology no longer wants to be a science of the "soul" but rather of "psychical phenomena." If that is what it wants, then it must be able to describe and determine these phenomena with conceptual rigor. It must have acquired the necessary rigorous concepts by methodical work. Where is this methodical work accomplished in "exact" psychology? We seek for it in vain throughout its vast literature. . . .

Only the spatio-temporal world of bodies is nature in the significant sense of that word. All other individual being, i.e. the psychical, is nature in a secondary sense, a fact which determines basically essential differences between the methods of natural science and psychology. In principle only corporeal being can be experienced in a number of direct experiences, i.e. perceptions, as individually identical. Hence, only this being can, if the perceptions are thought of as distributed among various "subjects," be experienced by many subjects as individually identical and be described as intersubjectively the same. The same realities (things, procedures, etc.), are present to the eyes of all and can be determined by us all according to their "nature." Their "nature" however denotes: presenting themselves in experience according to diversely varying "subjective appearances." . . .

Now, to what extent is something like rational investigation and valid statement possible in this sphere? To what extent too are only such statements possible which we have just now given as most crude descriptions (passing over in silence entire dimensions)? Now evidently research will here be meaningful, when precisely it surrenders itself purely to the sense of experiences, which are given as experiences of the "psychical," and when thereby it accepts and tries to determine the "psychical" exactly as it demands, as it were, to be accepted and determined, when it is viewed—above all where one does not allow absurd naturalizing. One must, it was said, take phenomena as they give themselves, i.e. as this flowing having-consciousness, intending, appearing, which they are, as this foreground and background having-consciousness, a having-consciousness as present or pre-present, as imagined or symbolic or derived, as intuitive or represented emptily, etc. Thus, too, they are to be taken in the variation of this or that point of view, this or that mode of attention turning now one way, now another, and transforming itself. All that bears the title "consciousness-of" and has a "meaning" and "intends" something "objective," which latter—whether from one standpoint or other it is to be called "fiction" or "reality"—permits being described as something "immanently objective," "intended as such," and intended in one or another mode of intending.

That one can here investigate and enunciate, and do so on the basis of evidence, adapting oneself to the sense of this sphere of "experience," is absolutely evident. It is, precisely, fidelity to the demands indicated above which constitutes the difficulty. On the single-mindedness and purity of the "phenomenological" attitude depends entirely the consistency or absurdity of the investigations which are here to be carried out. We do not easily overcome the inborn habit of living and thinking according to the naturalistic attitude, and thus of naturalistically falsifying the psychical. Furthermore, overcoming this habit depends to a great extent on the insight that in fact a "purely immanent" investigation of the psychical (using the term in its widest sense which means the phenomenal as such) is possible, the kind of research which has just been generally characterized and which stands in contrast to any psycho-physical investigation of the same, the latter being a kind of investigation we have not yet taken into consideration and which, of course, has its justification.

RICHARD MCKEON

Philosophy and Method

Richard McKeon (1900–) was born in New Jersey. His A.B., M.A., and Ph.D. degrees all come from Columbia University, where he taught for ten years before going to the University of Chicago. At Chicago, McKeon has taught history and Greek as well as philosophy. He has frequently participated in international cultural and philosophical meetings, and has published a number of books on the history of philosophy, metaphysics, and the structure of philosophical thought.

The methods of philosophy are methods of statement and of action. . . . The numerous methods that have been elaborated may be classified under three heads as methods of *dialectic*, of *logistic*, and of *inquiry*. Such a classification depends, however, on a strict statement of the differences of these methods, for within the framework of each method the others are assigned a subordinate place which is sometimes important and sometimes trivial. In a dialectical philosophy, dialectic is a method of proof and inquiry, and dialectic is employed even for the more restricted objectives of formal logic and experimental methodology. In a logistic calculus such validity as dialectic and the methods of inquiry possess can be expressed in formal arguments. In a philosophy of inquiry and discovery, dialectic and logistic are abstract forms unless given content by the results of inquiry.

The dialectical method—which has assumed many guises from its application by Parmenides [1] and Plato to Being and Forms to its application in contemporary transformations of Hegelianism and Marxism to Spirit and Matter—is adapted to the conflicts and contradictions found in nature, experience, knowledge, and action. The various forms of dialectic have in common, therefore, the purpose

From Richard McKeon, "Philosophy and Method," *The Journal of Philosophy*, **XLVIII**, No. 22 (1951), pp. 653–683. Reprinted by permission of publisher and author.

[1] Parmenides (6th–5th century B.C.) argued that ordinary experience is contradictory and that all that really exists is just Being itself.—Ed.

to transcend or remove contradictions as they are eliminated in the processes of nature, in the sequence of history, or in the insights of art, the stages of scientific thought, or the interplay of group inquiry in conversation. All forms of the dialectical method implicate in some fashion the impossibility of independent finite substances, of clear and distinct ideas, and of fixed univocal definitions, since all things, all thoughts, and all processes and statements are influenced by the organic wholes of which they are dependent parts and in which they are distinguishable only momentarily and as a consequences of analysis. Dialectical philosophies tend therefore to construct the sciences into a unified whole in which all forms of knowledge are arranged in hierarchy, or at least a dichotomy, according to their certainty and in an order according to the sequence of their development. In that unity the arts and the sciences are strictly comparable in contents, forms, and effects. The most certain science is also the most inclusive; that science is dialectic and it is the foundation to, as well as the method of, all other arts and sciences.

The logistic method has likewise assumed many forms, beginning with the early evidence of its existence found in the unsympathetic description of it by Plato and continuing through the construction of atomisms, logical terminisms, speculative grammars, and mathematical systems, to the elaborations of symbolic logic based on recent studies of the processes of mathematical proof. Whereas the dialectical method is adapted to transform and transcend the contradictions of nature, experience, knowledge, and action, the logistic method is adapted to trace knowledge back to the elements of which it is composed and the processes by which they are related. Those elements and their simple processes may be found in things, in thoughts, or in symbols. The atoms and void of Democritus,[2] the clear, distinct, and adequate ideas of Descartes and Leibniz,[3] or the simple ideas and the historical, plain method of Locke,[4] and the

[2] Democritus (5th–4th century B.C.) attempted to account for everything in terms of the arrangement and movement of atoms.—Ed.

[3] Gottfried Wilhelm von Leibniz (1646–1716) proposed to base all knowledge on a few ideas regarded as unquestionable.—Ed.

[4] John Locke (1632–1704) thought that all our knowledge could be derived from "simple" ideas arising in sensation and reflection.—Ed.

signs and rules of operation of modern symbolic logic are variant forms of the logistic method. If one begins with material particles and their motions, thought and language are phenomena which can be explained by material organic processes. If one begins with long chains of reasoning in which simple and indivisible ideas are ordered by simple relations or with systematic analyses in which complex ideas and modes are analyzed into their elements, scientific knowledge of nature and all modes of expression can be explained relatively to the bases found for them in ideas. If one begins with clearly defined symbols and clearly formulated operations, the knowledge of nature can be systematized by formalizing the language of science and there is no need for a separate consideration of thought.

Something of the complexity of the relations of the basic methods of philosophy can be seen in the fact that dialectic in its various forms and logistic in its various forms both claim the support of the natural sciences and both profess to use the methods of mathematics, but the mathematics of dialectic takes its examples from topology and projective geometry and its science is drawn from the reductions and analogies made possible by theories like those of relativity physics and from the applications of technology, while the logistic method centers on the postulational techniques of geometry and arithmetic and on laws which take forms similar to those of the various branches of mechanics.

All forms of the logistic method implicate, whatever the basic elements and processes employed, the necessity of univocal definitions based on indivisible particles, simple ideas, or arbitrary signs, and of simple processes and relations which govern their organization into systems. Logistic philosophies tend therefore to rearrange the sciences into a unified whole deduced in sequence from common primitive definitions and assumptions to which additional elements and processes are joined to construct more derived and more complex sciences. In that unified science, however, knowledge can be formalized only after a science has been sufficiently developed to be capable of formal statement, and whatever is non-cognitive in art and in action, in ordinary language and in everyday life falls outside the scope of the logistic method, except in indirect application insofar as those phenomena are analyzed according to the laws of some science or according to the calculation of probabilities.

The method of inquiry assumes many forms in philosophies which seek methods appropriate to the varieties of problems encountered in life, in art, and in science. The objective of the method of inquiry is neither the resolution of contrarieties into more inclusive or posterior dialectical unities nor the organization of more and more sciences into systems of deductive consequences from primitive principles, but the discovery of solutions of problems and the advancement of knowledge. The method of inquiry, therefore, is a plurality of methods: a general logic common to all the sciences and particular methods adapted to the problems, the subject-matters, and the principles of the particular sciences. . . .

The methods of dialectic, of logistic, and of inquiry are processes which differ so radically that they completely transform the contents, forms, and purposes of philosophy. Yet they are so closely related that the same statements can be repeated and seem to refer to the same subject-matter and problems and yet have meanings so different in dialectic, in logistic, and in inquiry that a vast portion of philosophical literature is devoted to pointing out the absurdities which no one could fail to recognize in what philosophers have said. The radical differences concerning substance and being, existence and essence, knowledge and belief, idea and impression, inference and implication, proposition and symbol, although they are not sufficient to obscure wholly the good sense and importance of what philosophers have said on these subjects, remove even the semblance of continuity from the history of philosophical systems and from the discussion of philosophical problems. . . .

The relations among philosophies are not simple differences concerning the same or comparable problems, nor can they be reduced to a translation formula which will transform a philosophic doctrine into the equivalent statement proper to another philosophy. Problems and doctrines move from subject-matter to subject-matter; even within a single subject-matter they take on different meanings and purposes from different principles; and subject-matters and principles are transformed by alterations of method. The subject-matter of philosophy is universal, and there is no reason *a priori* why any starting-point should provide better principles than any other or why any method adapted to the scope and intricacies of a universal subject should be preferable to any other. The sciences, the arts, the moral virtues, and the forms of polity afford neither analogies nor guidance for the resolution of this ultimate problem, since they are conceived and enter discussion in forms determined by philosophical principles and methods. . . .

Differences of methods, principles, purposes, and subject-matters account at once for the richness of philosophic discussion and the impossibility of bringing it to an unambiguous termination. The natural tendency to think in some one form or derivative of dialectic, logistic, or inquiry is strengthened by the facility of interpreting anything that is said in accordance with other methods in meanings, sometimes fantastic and often false, determined by one's own mode of thought. The fact that what seem common principles are applied by different methods to different subjects for different purposes easily escapes attention, since philosophers assume that the statements which result from their methods and purposes are as universal as their subject-matter.

R. G. COLLINGWOOD

Question and Answer

Robin George Collingwood (1889–1943) was taught by his father until he was thirteen years old. He began studying Latin at four and Greek at six. He was formally educated first at Rugby and then at Oxford, where he later became Professor of Philosophy. He was a noted authority on the Roman occupation of Britain as well as a philosopher, and wrote several books on the subject. He also translated the works of some Italian philosophers into English. His own philosophical books number about a dozen. Espousing a point of view that was no longer popular among his colleagues, Collingwood was philosophically a lone wolf, and perhaps commands more attention today than he did in his own time.

You cannot find out what a man means by simply studying his spoken or written statements, even though he has spoken or written with perfect command of language and perfectly truthful intention. In order to find out his meaning you must also know what the question was (a question in his own mind, and presumed by him to be in yours) to which the thing he has said or written was meant as an answer.

It must be understood that question and answer, as I conceived them, were strictly correlative. A proposition was not an answer, or at any rate could not be the right answer, to any question which might have been answered otherwise. A highly detailed and particularized proposition must be the answer, not to a vague and generalized question, but to a question as detailed and particularized as itself. For example, if my car will not go, I may spend an hour searching for the cause of its failure. If, during this hour, I take out number one plug, lay it on the engine, turn the starting-handle, and watch for a spark, my observation 'number one plug is all right' is an answer not to the question, 'Why won't my car go?' but to the question, 'Is it because number one plug is not sparking that my car

Taken from R. G. Collingwood, *An Autobiography* (New York: Oxford University Press, 1939), pp. 31–42, 60–64, *passim.* Used by permission of the Clarendon Press, Oxford.

won't go?' Any one of the various experiments I make during the hour will be the finding of an answer to some such detailed and particularized question. The question, 'Why won't my car go?' is only a kind of summary of all these taken together. It is not a separate question asked at a separate time, nor is it a sustained question which I continue to ask for the whole hour together. Consequently, when I say 'Number one plug is all right', this observation does not record one more failure to answer the hour-long question, 'What is wrong with my car?' It records a success in answering the three-minutes-long question, 'Is the stoppage due to failure in number one plug?'

In passing, I will note (what I shall return to later on) that this principle of correlativity between question and answer disposes of a good deal of clap-trap. People will speak of a savage as 'confronted by the eternal problem of obtaining food'. But what really confronts him is the problem, quite transitory like all things human, of spearing this fish, or digging up this root, or finding blackberries in this wood.

My next step was to apply this principle to the idea of contradiction. The current logic maintained that two propositions might, simply as propositions, contradict one another, and that by examining them simply as propositions you could find out whether they did so or not. This I denied. If you cannot tell what a proposition means unless you know what question it is meant to answer, you will mistake its meaning if you make a mistake about that question. One symptom of mistaking the meaning of a proposition is thinking that it contradicts another proposition which in fact it does not contradict. No two propositions, I saw, can contradict one another unless they are answers to the same question. It is therefore impossible to say of a man, 'I do not know what the question is which he is trying to answer, but I can see that he is contradicting himself'.

The same principle applied to the idea of truth. If the meaning of a proposition is relative to the question it answers, its truth must be relative to the same thing. Meaning, agreement and contradiction, truth and falsehood, none of these belonged to propositions in their own right, propositions by themselves; they belonged only to propositions as the answers to questions: each proposition answering a question strictly correlative to itself.

Here I parted company with what I called propositional logic, and its offspring the generally recognized theories of truth. According to propositional logic (under which denomination I include the so-called 'traditional' logic, the 'idealistic' logic of the eighteenth and nineteenth centuries, and the 'symbolic' logic of the nineteenth and twentieth), truth or falsehood, which are what logic is chiefly concerned with, belongs to propositions as such. This doctrine was often expressed by calling the proposition the 'unit of thought', meaning that if you divide it up into parts such as subject, copula, predicate, any of these parts taken singly is not a complete thought, that is, not capable of being true or false. . . .

For a logic of propositions I wanted to substitute what I called a logic of question and answer. It seemed to me that truth, if that meant the kind of thing which I was accustomed to pursue in my ordinary work as a philosopher or historian—truth in the sense in which a philosophical theory or an historical narrative is called true, which seemed to me the proper sense of the word—was something that belonged not to any single proposition, nor even, as the coherence-theorists maintained, to a complex of propositions taken together; but to a complex consisting of questions and answers. The structure of this complex had, of course, never been studied by propositional logic; but with help from Bacon,[1] Descartes, and others I could hazard a few statements about it. Each question and each answer in a given complex had to be relevant or appropriate, had to 'belong' both to the whole and to the place it occupied in the whole. Each question had to 'arise'; there must be that about it whose absence we condemn when we refuse to answer a question on the ground that it 'doesn't arise'. Each answer must be 'the right' answer to the question it professes to answer. . . .

What is ordinarily meant when a proposition is called 'true', I thought, was this: (*a*) the proposition belongs to a question-and-answer complex which as a whole is 'true' in the proper sense of the word; (*b*) within this complex it is an answer to a certain question; (*c*) the question is what we ordinarily call a sensible or intelligent

[1] Francis Bacon (1561–1626) was an English philosopher who contended that the thinking of most people is distorted by their prejudices and preconceptions.—Ed.

question, not a silly one, or in my terminology it 'arises'; (*d*) the proposition is the 'right' answer to that question.

If this is what is meant by calling a proposition 'true', it follows not only that you cannot tell whether a proposition is 'true' or 'false' until you know what question it was intended to answer, but also that a proposition which in fact is 'true' can always be thought 'false' by any one who takes the trouble to excogitate a question to which it would have been the wrong answer, and convinces himself that this was the question it was meant to answer. And a proposition which in fact is significant can always be thought meaningless by any one who convinces himself that it was intended as an answer to a question which, if it had really been intended to answer it, it would not have answered at all, either rightly or wrongly. Whether a given proposition is true or false, significant or meaningless, depends on what question it was meant to answer; and any one who wishes to know whether a given proposition is true or false, significant or meaningless, must find out what question it was meant to answer.

Now, the question 'To what question did So-and-so intend this proposition for an answer?' is an historical question, and therefore cannot be settled except by historical methods. When So-and-so wrote in a distant past, it is generally a very difficult one, because writers (at any rate good writers) always write for their contemporaries, and in particular for those who are 'likely to be interested', which means those who are already asking the question to which an answer is being offered; and consequently a writer very seldom explains what the question is that he is trying to answer. Later on, when he has become a 'classic' and his contemporaries are all long dead, the question has been forgotten; especially if the answer he gave was generally acknowledged to be the right answer; for in that case people stopped asking the question, and began asking the question that next arose. So the question asked by the original writer can only be reconstructed historically, often not without the exercise of considerable historical skill. . . .

It follows, too, and this is what especially struck me at the time, that whereas no two propositions can be in themselves mutually contradictory, there are many cases in which one and the same pair of propositions are capable of being thought either that or the opposite, according as the questions they were meant to answer are reconstructed in one way or in another. For example, metaphysicians have been heard to say 'the world is both one and many'; and critics have not been wanting who were stupid enough to accuse them of contradicting themselves, on the abstractly logical ground that 'the world is one' and 'the world is many' are mutually contradictory propositions. A great deal of the popular dislike of metaphysics is based on grounds of this sort, and is ultimately due to critics who, as we say, did not know what the men they criticized were talking about; that is, did not know what questions their talk was intended to answer; but, with the ordinary malevolence of the idle against the industrious, the ignorant against the learned, the fool against the wise man, wished to have it believed that they were talking nonsense.

Suppose, instead of talking about the world, the metaphysician were talking about the contents of a small mahogany box with a sliding top; and suppose he said, 'The contents of this box are both one thing and many things'. A stupid critic may think that he is offering two incompatible answers to a single question, 'Are the contents of this box *x* or many *x*'s?' But the critic has reconstructed the question wrong. There were two questions: (*a*) Are the contents of this box one set of chessmen or many sets? (*b*) Are the contents of this box one chessman or many chessmen?

There is no contradiction between saying that something, whether that something be the world or the contents of a box, is one, and saying that it is many. Contradiction would set in only if that something were said to be both one *x* and many *x*'s. But in the original statement, whether about the world or about the chessmen, there was nothing about one *x* and many *x*'s. That was foisted upon it by the critic. The contradiction of which the critic complains never existed in his victim's philosophy at all, until the critic planted it upon him, as he might have planted treasonable correspondence in his coat pockets; and with an equally laudable intention, to obtain a reward for denouncing him.

Thus, if a given doctrine D is criticized as self-contradictory because it is divisible into two parts E and F, where E contradicts F, the criticism is valid only if the critic has correctly reconstructed the questions to which E and F were given as answers. A critic who is aware of this condition will of course 'show his working' by stating to his readers the evidence on which he has concluded that the author criticized really did formulate his questions in such a way that E and F in his mouth were mutually contradictory. Failing that, a reader disinclined to work the problem out for himself will naturally assume the criticism to be sound or unsound according as he has found the critic to be, in a general way, a good historian or a bad one. . . .

During the War . . . I set myself to reconsider [the] 'realist' attitude towards the history of philosophy. Was it really true, I asked myself, that the problems of philosophy were, even in the loosest sense of that word, eternal? Was it really true that different philosophies were different attempts to answer the same questions? I soon discovered that it was not true; it was merely a vulgar error, consequent on a kind of historical myopia which, deceived by superficial resemblances, failed to detect profound differences.

The first point at which I saw a perfectly clear gleam of daylight was in political theory. Take Plato's *Republic* and Hobbes's *Leviathan,* so far as they are concerned with politics. Obviously the political theories they set forth are not the same. But do they represent two different theories of the same thing? Can you say that the *Republic* gives one account of 'the nature of the State' and the *Leviathan* another? No; because Plato's 'State' is the Greek πόλις,[2] and Hobbes's is the absolutist State of the seventeenth century. The 'realist' answer is easy: certainly Plato's State is different from Hobbes's, but they are both States; so the theories are theories of the State. Indeed, what did you mean by calling them both political, if not that they were theories of the same thing?

It was obvious to me that this was only a piece of logical bluff, and that if instead of logic-chopping you got down to brass tacks and called for definitions of the 'State' as Plato conceived it and as Hobbes conceived it, you would find that the differences between them were not superficial but went down to essentials. You can call the two things the same if you insist; but if you do, you must admit that the thing has got *diablement changé en route,* so that the 'nature

[2] The *polis* was the city-state which typified ancient Greek political organization.—Ed.

of the State' in Plato's time was genuinely different from the 'nature of the State' in Hobbes's. I do not mean the empirical nature of the State; I mean the ideal nature of the State. What even the best and wisest of those who are engaged in politics are trying to do has altered. Plato's *Republic* is an attempt at a theory of one thing; Hobbes's *Leviathan* an attempt at a theory of something else.

There is, of course, a connexion between these two things; but it is not the kind of connexion that the 'realists' thought it was. Anybody would admit that Plato's *Republic* and Hobbes's *Leviathan* are about two things which are in one way the same thing and in another way different. That is not in dispute. What is in dispute is the kind of sameness and the kind of difference. The 'realists' thought that the sameness was the sameness of a 'universal', and the difference the difference between two instances of that universal. But this is not so. The sameness is the sameness of an historical process, and the difference is the difference between one thing which in the course of that process has turned into something else, and the other thing into which it has turned. Plato's πόλις and Hobbes's absolutist State are related by a traceable historical process, whereby one has turned into the other; any one who ignores that process, denies the difference between them, and argues that where Plato's political theory contradicts Hobbes's one of them must be wrong, is saying the thing that is not.

Pursuing this line of inquiry, I soon realized that the history of political theory is not the history of different answers given to one and the same question, but the history of a problem more or less constantly changing, whose solution was changing with it. The 'form of the πόλις' is not, as Plato seems to have thought, the one and only ideal of human society possible to intelligent men. It is not something eternally laid up in heaven and eternally envisaged, as the goal of their efforts, by all good statesmen of whatever age and country. It was the ideal of human society as that ideal was conceived by the Greeks of Plato's own time. By the time of Hobbes, people had changed their minds not only about what was possible in the way of social organization, but about what was desirable. Their ideals were different. And consequently the political philosophers whose business it was to give a reasoned statement of these ideals had a different task before them; one which, if it was to be rightly discharged, must be discharged differently.

The clue, once found, was easily applied elsewhere. It was not difficult to see that, just as the Greek πόλις could not be legitimately translated by the modern word 'State', except with a warning that the two things are in various essential ways different, and a statement of what these differences are; so, in ethics, a Greek word like δεῖ cannot be legitimately translated by using the word 'ought', if that word carries with it the notion of what is sometimes called 'moral obligation'. Was there any Greek word or phrase to express that notion? The 'realists' said there was; but they stultified themselves by adding that the 'theories of moral obligation' expounded by Greek writers differed from modern theories such as Kant's about the same thing. How did they know that the Greek and the Kantian theories were about the same thing? Oh, because δεῖ (or whatever word it was) is the Greek for 'ought'.

It was like having a nightmare about a man who had got it into his head that τριήρης [3] was the Greek for 'steamer', and when it was pointed out to him that descriptions of triremes in Greek writers were at any rate not very good descriptions of steamers, replied triumphantly, 'That is just what I say. These Greek philosophers' (or, 'these modern philosophers', according to which side he was on in the good old controversy between the Ancients and the Moderns) 'were terribly muddle-headed, and their theory of steamers is all wrong'. If you tried to explain that τριήρης does not mean steamer at all but something different, he would reply, 'Then what does it mean?' and in ten minutes he would show you that you didn't know; you couldn't draw a trireme, or make a model of one, or even describe exactly how it worked. And having annihilated you, he would go on for the rest of his life translating τριήρης 'steamer'.

If he had not been quite so clever, he might have known that by a careful sifting and interpretation of the evidence you can arrive at some conclusions, though certainly incomplete ones, about what a trireme was like. And by similar treatment of the evidence you can arrive at some conclusions about the meaning of words like δεῖ.

[3] *Triērēs,* literally "trireme."—Ed.

But in both cases you have to approach the matter from an historical point of view, not from that of a minute philosopher; and in the conviction that whatever the Greek word in question means it will not necessarily (indeed, not probably) mean anything that can be rendered by one word, if indeed by any words, in English.

MARTIN HEIDEGGER

What Is Philosophy?

Martin Heidegger (1889–) was born in the Black Forest of Germany and brought up as a Roman Catholic. Although he left the Church as a young man, the continued effect it had upon his thought is shown by the fact that an early book of his concerns the doctrines of Duns Scotus, a medieval scholar. As a student and later instructor at the University of Freiburg, Heidegger also came under the influence of Edmund Husserl, the phenomenologist. Heidegger later became professor of philosophy of Marburg. It was here that he wrote his greatest book Sein und Zeit (Being and Time). *When Husserl retired, Heidegger was named his successor at Freiburg. Under the Nazi regime he was made Rector of this University in 1933, but he resigned this post the following year. Since then he has been living in the Black Forest, whence he has from time to time emerged to teach at Freiburg.*

With this question we are touching on a theme which is very broad, that is, widespread. Because the theme is broad, it is indefinite. Because it is indefinite, we can treat the theme from the most varied points of view. Thereby we shall always hit upon something that is valid. But because, in the treatment of this extensive theme, all possible opinions intermingle, we are in danger of having our discussion lack proper cohesion.

Therefore, we must try to define the question more exactly. In this manner we direct the discussion into a definite direction. The discussion is thereby brought into a path. I say—into *a* path. Thereby we admit that this path is certainly not the only one. It must, in fact, remain open whether the path which I should like to indicate in what follows is, in truth, a path which allows us to pose and answer the question.

If we now assume that we might find a way of determining the question more exactly, then there immediately arises a grave objection to the theme of our discussion. When we ask, "What is philos-

From Martin Heidegger, *What Is Philosophy?*, translated from the German by William Kluback and Jean T. Wilde (New York: Twayne Publishers, Inc., 1958), pp. 19–35, 67–85, 89–97. Used by permission of Twayne Publishers.

ophy?" then we are speaking *about* philosophy. By asking in this way we are obviously taking a stand above and, therefore, outside of philosophy. But the aim of our question is to enter *into* philosophy, to tarry in it, to conduct ourselves in its manner, that is, to "philosophize." The path of our discussion must, therefore, not only have a clear direction, but this direction must at the same time give us the guarantee that we are moving within philosophy and not outside of it and around it.

The path of our discussion must, therefore, be of such a kind and direction that that of which philosophy treats concerns us personally, affects us and, indeed, touches us in our very nature.

But does not philosophy thereby become a matter of affection, emotions, and sentiments?

"With fine sentiments bad literature is made."[1] These words of André Gide apply not only to literature but even more to philosophy. Sentiments, even the finest, have no place in philosophy. Sentiments, it is said, are something irrational. Philosophy, on the other hand, is not only something rational but is the actual guardian of reason. In making this assertion we have come unawares to a kind of decision as to what philosophy is. We have already anticipated our question with an answer. Everyone considers the assertion correct that philosophy is a matter of reason. However, this assertion is perhaps a premature and hasty answer to the question, "What is philosophy?" for we can immediately oppose new questions to this answer. What is reason? Where and through whom was it decided what reason is? Has reason constituted itself to be the ruler of philosophy? If so, by what right? If not, whence does it obtain its mission and its role? If what is considered to be reason was first established only by philosophy and within the course of its history, then it is not good judgment to proclaim philosophy in advance as a matter of reason. However, as soon as we cast doubt on the characterization of philosophy as rational behavior, then in the same way it also becomes questionable whether philosophy belongs in the domain of the irrational. For whoever wishes to designate philosophy as irrational thereby takes the rational as a measure of limitation and, what is more, does it in such a way as again to take for granted what reason is.

[1] André Gide, *Dostoievsky* (Paris: Plon-Nourrit, 1923), p. 247.

If, on the other hand, we point out the possibility that that upon which philosophy bears concerns us humans in our essential nature and moves [2] us, then it might be that this being-moved has nothing whatsoever to do with that which is usually called feelings and emotions, in short, the irrational.

From what has been said, we deduce at first only this one thing: greater care is required if we hazard a discussion under the title "What is Philosophy?"

The first thing for us to do is to lead the question to a clearly directed path so that we do not flounder around in either convenient or haphazard conceptions of philosophy. But how are we to find a path by which we can determine our question reliably?

The path which I should now like to point out lies directly before us. And only because it is the nearest at hand is it difficult to find. However, when we have found it, we still move along it awkwardly. We ask, "What is philosophy?" We have uttered the word "philosophy" often enough. If, however, we use the word "philosophy" no longer like a wornout title, if, instead, we hear the word "philosophy" coming from its source, then it sounds thus: *philosophia.* Now the word "philosophy" is speaking Greek. The word, as a Greek word, is a path. This path, on the one hand, lies before us, for the word has long since been spoken, i.e. set forth. On the other hand, it lies behind us, for we have always heard and spoken this word. Accordingly, the Greek word *philosophia* is a path along which we are traveling. Yet we have only a vague knowledge of this path although we possess and can spread much historical information about Greek philosophy.

The word *philosophia* tells us that philosophy is something which, first of all, determines the existence of the Greek world. Not only that—*philosophia* also determines the innermost basic feature of our Western-European history. The often heard expression "Western-European philosophy" is, in truth, a tautology. Why? Because philosophy is Greek in its nature; Greek, in this instance, means that in origin the nature of philosophy is of such a kind that it first appropriated the Greek world, and only it, in order to unfold.

[2] *be-rühren,* as Heidegger uses it here, indicates not an emotional stirring but a metaphysical stirring, consequently, not an affection but an essential movement.—Trans.

However, the originally Greek nature of philosophy, in the era of its modern-European sway, has been guided and ruled by Christian conceptions. The dominance of these conceptions was mediated by the Middle Ages. At the same time, one cannot say that philosophy thereby became Christian, that is, became a matter of belief in revelation and the authority of the Church. The statement that philosophy is in its nature Greek says nothing more than that the West and Europe, and only these, are, in the innermost course of their history, originally "philosophical." This is attested by the rise and dominance of the sciences. Because they stem from the innermost Western-European course of history, that is, the philosophical, consequently they are able, today, to put a specific imprint on the history of mankind upon the whole earth.

Let us consider for a moment what it means that an era in the history of mankind is characterized as the "atomic age." The atomic energy discovered and liberated by the sciences is represented as that force which is to determine the course of history. Indeed, there would never have been any sciences if philosophy had not preceded them and proceeded. But philosophy is *the philosophia.* This Greek word binds our discussion to an historical tradition. Because this tradition is of a unique kind, it is also unique in meaning. This tradition which bears the Greek name *philosophia,* and which is labelled for us with the historical word *philosophia,* reveals the direction of a path on which we ask, "What is philosophy?" Tradition does not surrender us to a constraint by what is past and irrevocable. Surrendering is a delivering into the freedom of discussion with what has been. If we truly hear the word and reflect upon what we have heard, the name "philosophy" summons us into the history of the Greek origin of philosophy. The word *philosophia* appears, as it were, on the birth certificate of our own history; we may even say on the birth certificate of the contemporary epoch of world history which is called the atomic age. That is why we can ask the question, "What is philosophy?" only if we enter into a discussion with the thinking of the Greek world. . . .

When is the answer to the question, "What is philosophy?" a philosophizing one? When do we philosophize? Obviously only when we enter into a discussion with philosophers. This implies that we talk through with them that about which they speak. This mutual talking through of what always anew peculiarly concerns philosophers as being the Same, that is talking, *legein,* in the sense of *dialegethai* [conversing], is talking as dialogue. If and when dialogue is necessarily dialectic, we leave open.

It is one thing to determine and describe the opinions of philosophers. It is an entirely different thing to talk through with them what they are saying, and that means, that of which they speak.

Thus, if we assume that the Being of being addresses itself to philosophers to the extent that they state what being is, in so far as it is, then our discussion with philosophers must also be addressed by the Being of being. We must then ourselves, through our thinking, go to meet philosophy on the path it is traveling. Our speaking must co-respond to that which addresses the philosophers. If this co-responding is successful for us, then, in the true sense of the word, we respond to the question, "What is philosophy?" The German word *antwòrten* [answer to] actually means the same as *entsprechen* [to respond]. The answer to our question is not exhausted in an affirmation which answers to the question by determining what we are to understand by the concept "philosophy." The answer is not a reply (*n'est pas une réponse*), the ańswer is rather the co-respondence (*la correspondance*) which responds to the Being of being. Yet, we should like at the same time to know what constitutes the characteristic feature of the answer in the sense of co-respondence. But everything first depends upon our attaining a co-respondence before we set up a theory about it.

The answer to the question, "What is philosophy?" consists in our corresponding to [answering to] that towards which philosophy is on the way. And that is—the Being of being. In such a correspondence we listen from the very outset to that which philosophy has already said to us, *philosophy,* that is, *philosophia* understood in the Greek sense. That is why we attain correspondence, that is, an answer to our question, only *when* we remain in conversation with that to which the tradition of philosophy delivers us, that is, liberates us. We find the answer to the question, "What is philosophy?" not through historical assertions about the definitions of philosophy but through conversing with that which has been handed down to us as the Being of being.

This path to the answer to our question is not a break with history, no repudiation of history, but is an adoption and transformation of what has been handed down to us. Such an adoption of history is what is meant by the term "destruction." The meaning of this word has been clearly described in *Sein und Zeit* (§6). Destruction does not mean destroying but dismantling, liquidating, putting to one side the merely historical assertions about the history of philosophy. Destruction means—to open our ears, to make ourselves free for what speaks to us in tradition as the Being of being. By listening to this interpellation we attain the correspondence.

But while we are saying this, a doubt has already made itself felt. It is this—must we first make an effort to reach a correspondence with the Being of being? Are we, humans, not always already in such a correspondence, and, what is more, not only *de facto,* but by virtue of our nature? Does not this correspondence constitute the fundamental trait of our nature?

This is, indeed, the case. But if this is the case, then we can no longer say that we first have to attain this correspondence. And yet we are right in saying so. For, to be sure, although we do remain always and everywhere in correspondence to the Being of being, we, nevertheless, rarely pay attention to the appeal of Being. The correspondence to the Being of being does, to be sure, always remain our abode. But only at times does it become an unfolding attitude specifically adopted by us. Only when this happens do we really correspond to that which concerns philosophy which is on the way towards the Being of being. Philosophy is the correspondence to the Being of being, but not until, and only when, the correspondence is actually fulfilled and thereby unfolds itself and expands this unfoldment. This correspondence occurs in different ways according to how the appeal of Being speaks, according to whether it is heard or not heard, and according to whether what is heard is said or is kept silent. Our discussion can result in opportunities to reflect upon it.

Now I shall only try to express a foreword to the discussion. I should like to turn the discussion back to what we touched upon in connection with André Gide's words about "fine sentiments." *Philosophia* is the expressly accomplished correspondence which speaks in so far as it considers the appeal of the Being of being. The correspondence listens to the voice of the appeal. What appeals to us as the voice of Being evokes our correspondence. "Correspondence" then means: being de-termined, *être disposé* by that which comes from the Being of being. *Dis-posé* here means literally set-apart, cleared, and thereby placed in relationship with what is. Being as such determines speaking in such a way that language is attuned (*accorder*) to the Being of being. Correspondence is necessary and is always attuned, and not just accidentally and occasionally. It is in an attunement. And only on the basis of the attunement (*disposition*) does the language of correspondence obtain its precision, its tuning.

As something tuned and attuned, correspondence really exists in a tuning.[3] Through it our attitude is adjusted sometimes in this, sometimes in that way. The tuning understood in this sense is not music of accidentally emerging feelings which only accompany the correspondence. If we characterize philosophy as tuned correspondence, then we by no means want to surrender thinking to the accidental changes and vacillations of sentiments. It is rather solely a question of pointing out that every precision of language is grounded in a disposition of correspondence, of correspondence, I say, in heeding the appeal.

Above all, however, the reference to the essential disposition of correspondence is not a modern invention. The Greek thinkers, Plato and Aristotle, already drew attention to the fact that philosophy and philosophizing belong in the dimension of man which we call tuning (in the sense of tuning and attunement).

Plato says (*Theatetus,* 155 d): "For this is especially the *pathos* [emotion] of a philosopher, to be astonished.[4] For there is no other beginning of *philosophia* than this." "Very much is this especially the *pathos* of a philosopher, namely, to be astonished; for there is no other determining point of departure for philosophy than this."

[3] The translation of the word *Stimmung* by tuning implies also the idea of disposition. Heidegger shows that it is necessary to be disposed, or tuned, to a thought to understand it. Philosophical concepts must be grasped. This is possible only if the mind is attuned or disposed for the grasping of the idea. Therefore, the word tuning implies disposition. It is this disposition or tuning which makes possible the Being of being.—Trans.

[4] The Greek verb *thaumazein,* which Heidegger translates "to be astonished," can also be translated "to wonder." Hence what Plato is saying here is that philosophy begins in wonder. See the Introduction to this book, p. 4.—Ed.

Astonishment, as *pathos*, is the *archê* [the beginning] of philosophy. We must understand the Greek word *archê* [beginning] in its fullest sense. It names that from which something proceeds. But this "from where" is not left behind in the process of going out, but the beginning rather becomes that which the verb *archein* expresses, that which governs. The *pathos* of astonishment thus does not simply stand at the beginning of philosophy, as, for example, the washing of his hands precedes the surgeon's operation. Astonishment carries and pervades philosophy.

Aristotle says the same thing (*Metaphysics* A 2, 982 b 12 sq): "For through astonishment men have begun to philosophize both in our times and at the beginning." "Through astonishment men have reached now, as well as at first, the determining path of philosophizing" (that from which philosophizing emanates and that which altogether determines the course of philosophizing).

It would be very superficial and, above all, very un-Greek, if we would believe that Plato and Aristotle are only determining here that astonishment is the cause of philosophizing. If they were of this opinion, that would mean that at some time or other men were astonished especially about being and that it is and what it is. Impelled by this astonishment, they began to philosophize. As soon as philosophy was in progress, astonishment became superfluous as a propelling force so that it disappeared. It could disappear since it was only an impetus. However, astonishment is *archê*—it pervades every step of philosophy. Astonishment is *pathos*. We usually translate *pathos* with passion, ebullition of emotion. But *pathos* is connected with *paschein*, to suffer, endure, undergo, to be borne along by, to be determined by. It is risky, as it always is in such cases, if we translate *pathos* with tuning, by which we mean dis-position and determination. But we must risk this translation because it alone protects us from conceiving *pathos* in a very modern psychological sense. Only if we understand *pathos* as being attuned to, can we also characterize *thaumazein*,[5] astonishment, more exactly. In astonishment we restrain ourselves (*être en arrêt*). We step back, as it were, from being, from the fact that it is as it is and not otherwise. And astonishment is not used up in this retreating from the Being

[5] See footnote 4, above.—Ed.

of being, but, as this retreating and self-restraining, it is at the same time forcibly drawn to and, as it were, held fast by that from which it retreats. Thus, astonishment is disposition in which and for which the Being of being unfolds. Astonishment is the tuning within which the Greek philosophers were granted the correspondence to the Being of being. . . .

It looks as though we were only posing historical questions. But, in truth, we are considering the future nature of philosophy. We are trying to listen to the voice of Being. Into what kind of tuning does this put contemporary thinking? The question can scarcely be answered unequivocally. Presumably a fundamental tuning prevails. It is, however, still hidden from us. This would indicate that our contemporary thinking has not yet found its unequivocal path. What we come across is only this—various tunings of thinking. Doubt and despair, on the one hand, blind obsession by untested principles, on the other, conflict with one another. Fear and anxiety are mixed with hope and confidence. Often and widely, it looks as though thinking were a kind of reasoning conception and calculation completely free of any kind of tuning. But even the coldness of calculation, even the prosaic sobriety of planning are traits of an attunement. Not only that—even reason, which keeps itself free of every influence of the passions, is, as reason, attuned to confidence in the logically mathematical intelligence of its principles and rules.

The expressly adopted and unfolding correspondence which corresponds to the appeal of the Being of being is philosophy. We are introduced to and become acquainted with what philosophy is only when we learn how, in what manner, it is. It is in the manner of correspondence which is attuned to the voice of the Being of being.

This corresponding is a speaking. It is in the service of *language.* What this means is difficult for us to understand today, for our current conception of language has undergone strange changes. As a consequence, language appears as an instrument of expression. Accordingly, it is considered more correct to say that language is in the service of thinking rather than that thinking, as co-respondence, is in the service of language. Above all, the current conception of language is as far removed as possible from the Greek experience of language. To the Greeks the nature of language is revealed as the *logos*.[6] But what do *logos* and *legein* mean? Only today are we slowly beginning to get a glimpse of its original Greek nature through the manifold interpretations of *logos*. However, we can neither ever again return to this nature of language, nor simply adopt it. On the contrary, we must probably enter into a conversation with the Greek experience of language as *logos*. Why? Because without a sufficient consideration of language, we never truly know what philosophy is as the distinguished co-respondence, nor what philosophy is as a distinctive manner of language.

But because poetry, if we compare it with thinking, is in the service of language in an entirely different and distinctive way, our discussion, which follows philosophy's thinking, necessarily leads to a discussion of the relationship between thinking and poetic creation. Between these two there exists a secret kinship because in the service of language both intercede on behalf of language and give lavishly of themselves. Between both there is, however, at the same time an abyss for they "dwell on the most widely separated mountains."

Now the request might quite justifiably be made that our discussion be restricted to the question about philosophy. This restriction would be possible and even necessary only if in the discussion it should turn out that philosophy is not that which it is now interpreted to be—a co-respondence which discusses the appeal of the Being of being.

In other words—our discussion does not set itself the task of winding up a fixed program. But it would like to prepare all who are participating for a gathering in which what we call the Being of being appeals to us. By naming this we are considering what Aristotle already says:

"Being-ness appears in many guises."[7] "Existence is revealed in many ways."

[6] The Greek noun, *logos* cannot be rendered by any single English word. "Reason," "thought," "definition," "speech," and "language" are among its meanings.—Ed.

[7] Cf. *Sein und Zeit*, §7B.

Bibliography

I. OLDER VIEWS OF THE NATURE OF PHILOSOPHY

Plato. *Republic,* 471c–509c. [A study of the role of the philosopher in an ideal society, and an account of the wisdom that he seeks.]

Aristotle. *Metaphysics,* Bk. Alpha, Chaps. 1–2. [A comparison of philosophical wisdom with other types of knowledge, and a statement of the main characteristics of such wisdom.]

St. Thomas Aquinas. *Summa Contra Gentiles,* Bk. I, Chaps. 3–13; and *Summa Theologica,* Part One, Question I. [Develops the relation between Faith and Reason in such a way as to make clear the position that "Philosophy is the handmaiden of theology."]

René Descartes. *Discourse on Method.* [A method for achieving rigor in philosophy and other theoretical inquiries.]

Immanuel Kant. *Prolegomena to Any Future Metaphysic.* [A discussion of the conditions under which knowledge is possible, and a critique of traditional philosophy.]

Georg Wilhelm Friedrich Hegel. *Phenomenology of Mind,* Preface. [A difficult but rewarding text in which Hegel considers the necessity of the philosophical enterprise and contrasts philosophy with other forms of knowledge.]

II. SOME ADDITIONAL CONTEMPORARY STATEMENTS REGARDING THE NATURE OF PHILOSOPHY

William James. *Pragmatism, a New Name for Some Old Ways of Thinking.* New York: Longmans, 1907. [A pragmatic approach to "the present dilemma in philosophy."]

C. D. Broad. *Scientific Thought.* New York: Harcourt, 1923, Introduction. [A noted advocate of analytic philosophy surveys the goals and methods of philosophy.]

Moritz Schlick. "The Turning Point in Philosophy" [reprinted in A. J. Ayer (ed.), *Logical Positivism.* Glencoe, Ill.: The Free Press, 1959, pp. 53–56.] [A definition of philosophy from the point of view of logical positivism, supplementing the Carnap selection in the present volume.]

Friedrich Waismann. "How I See Philosophy," in H. D. Lewis, *Contemporary British Philosophy,* Third Series. London: Allen & Unwin,

1956. [A sensitive examination of the techniques of the philosopher and of the relations between philosophy and other fields.]

W. B. Gallie. "Essentially Contested Concepts," *Proceedings of the Aristotelian Society*, 1956 (reprinted in Max Black, *The Importance of Language*. Englewood Cliffs, N.J.: Prentice-Hall, 1962). [An incisive study of philosophical disagreement.]

José Ortega y Gasset. *What Is Philosophy?* (trans. Mildred Adams). New York: Norton, 1960. [The answer that this Spanish existentialist gives is rambling but marked by insight.]

Henry W. Johnstone, Jr. *Philosophy and Argument.* University Park, Pa.: The Pennsylvania State Univ. Press, 1959.